DECISIONS, TECHNOLOGY AND ORGANIZATION

*Dedicated to friends, colleagues and students past and present, at Aston, Brunel, and Royal Holloway universities.*

# Decisions, Technology and Organization

AUDLEY GENUS
*School of Management, Royal Holloway,*
*University of London*

Routledge
Taylor & Francis Group
LONDON AND NEW YORK

First published 2000 by Gower Publishing

Reissued 2018 by Routledge
2 Park Square, Milton Park, Abingdon, Oxon OX14 4RN
711 Third Avenue, New York, NY 10017, USA

*Routledge is an imprint of the Taylor & Francis Group, an informa business*



A Library of Congress record exists under LC control number: 00110186

ISBN 13: 978-1-138-73064-9 (hbk)
ISBN 13: 978-1-138-73061-8 (pbk)
ISBN 13: 978-1-315-18934-5 (ebk)

# Contents

# List of Tables

# Preface

This short book draws on research on the problems of managing large-scale technology conducted by the author over the last decade. It addresses a persistent issue: the double-headed nature of grand projects involving technology. This is all too often revealed in the contrast between their hoped-for benefits and the optimism with which they are promoted, and the high human, economic or environmental costs of their operation. The book owes it inspiration to a body of work undertaken on the subject at the Technology Policy Unit at Aston University but seeks to connect this programme of research to wider developments within the social sciences. What follows therefore analyzes the construction of major technology projects taking in diverse contributions from political science, decision theory, the sociology of technology, and project management. As well being eclectic in its disciplinary orientation, the book attempts to capture the web of factors significant to the commitment that decision-makers maintain in the face of mounting difficulties with managing large-scale technology. It thus shuttles between the analysis of public policy level processes, the nature of government-industry relations, inter-firm contractual relationships, and the extent to which society in general is able to probe or assert influence over affairs that affect them. With regard to the latter the book aims to contribute to the development of a constructive relationship between technology development and social choice. Here, it builds upon the notion of 'creative incrementalism' advocated by proponents of constructive technology assessment as a means to improve the processes and choices made by society in the area of technology development, and to bring to the surface the values underpinning these. The book should be of interest to a wide range of researchers, practitioners and students at an advanced level in the disciplines identified above. Beyond these it will be of value to anyone with an interest in understanding and improving technology development and choice. The preparation of the manuscript has been informed by discussions with colleagues at the Technology Policy Unit at Aston University, within the Technology and Innovation Management group at Brunel University and at sessions at various international conferences and seminars. More specifically, I wish to thank the following: Steve Conway, Anne-Marie Coles, Keith Dickson,

Martin Harris, John Howells, Peter James, Christian Koch, Todd LaPorte, Ian McLoughlin, Ruth McNally, Harry Rothman, Fred Steward, and Ned Woodhouse. A special mention must go to my colleague David Collingridge, for his help and encouragement over the years.

Audley Genus

# Acknowledgements

The author wishes to acknowledge the support of the following: the ESRC and SERC for their joint support for research on the case of North Sea oil; Brunel University for funding the research that enabled the preparation of the Channel Tunnel case study; and Brendan Flynn for helping with the data collection on the Channel Tunnel project. The author also wishes to express his thanks to the following publishers for their permission to use excerpts of copyright material: Carfax, for the use of material on North Sea oil first published in Technology Analysis and Strategic Management, vol. 4, 1992, pp. 133-148; Elsevier, for the use of material on the Channel Tunnel, first published in Research Policy, vol. 26, 1997, pp. 169-189; and European Research Press, for the use of material on wave power, published in Business Strategy and the Environment, vol. 2, 1993, pp. 26-36.

# List of Abbreviations

| | |
|---|---|
| ACORD | Advisory Council on Research and Development |
| AGR | Advanced Gas Reactor |
| BNOC | British National Oil Corporation |
| CTA | Constructive Technology Assessment |
| CTG | Channel Tunnel Group |
| DETR | Department of the Environment, Transport and the Regions |
| ETSU | Energy Technology Support Unit |
| FM | Francemanche SA |
| IEA | International Energy Agency |
| IGC | Intergovernmental Commission |
| MdO | Maitre d'Oeuvre |
| NAO | National Audit Office |
| NASA | National Aeronautics and Space Administration |
| NETA | New Energy Trading Arrangements |
| NFFO | Non-fossil Fuel Obligation |
| OECD | Organization for Economic Cooperation and Development |
| OPEC | Organization of Petroleum Exporting Countries |
| PSBR | Public Sector Borrowing Requirement |
| TML | Transmanche Link |
| UKAEA | United Kingdom Atomic Energy Authority |
| UKCS | United Kingdom Continental Shelf |

# PART I
# INTRODUCTION

# 1 Perspectives and Prescriptions: the Analysis of Large-scale Technology

## Introduction

This book is about the theory and practice of decision-making and the construction of technology. It speaks to the poverty of attention to failed technological innovation identified by Pinch and Bijker (1987), which persists. It contributes to the literature on 'grand-scale' projects. Such projects provide society with some of its greatest enduring technical achievements but also with some of its most damaging or costly mistakes. Current illustrations of the type of ventures giving cause for concern include defence projects, which often incur very large cost overruns and long development delays (National Audit Office, 2000). Other contemporary projects such as dam-building schemes in Kurdish Turkey, the Oresundsbron road bridge linking Sweden and Denmark, or the Millennium Dome and Millennium Bridge further illustrate the potential ambivalence of large construction projects in terms of serving society. Critics attempt to sound their notes of caution. Supporters and promoters, however, point to the positive implications of these expenditures in terms of their contribution to domestic and foreign policy objectives. In the public debate, either heightened controversy ensues leading to inertia, or in the absence of criticism risky technology is 'pushed'. These observations are hardly new. Yet, surprisingly, there is relatively little research on public policy towards and the operational management of this type of venture. The study of grand projects is an area of research in need of further scrutiny, therefore (Shapira and Berndt, 1997).

In particular, it is necessary to examine what is meant by failure and success and to account for the factors promoting successful or unsuccessful large-scale technology projects. Some clues on the matter may be obtained by considering the merits of rival prescriptions for decision or policy-making, in conjunction with an analysis of technical, economic and organizational aspects of the major projects featured in the book. With this in mind, a further aim of the book is to bridge the gap between the prescriptive literature on decision-making, which tends to neglect the content and context of the phenomena in question, and histories and case studies of technology development, which eschew generalization in favour of description. To the extent that this occurs it will be possible to enhance our understanding of decision-making in complex or uncertain situations, the management and evaluation of grand projects, and the social construction of technology.

There are a number of concepts that are core to understanding processes of design, implementation and performance evaluation in these areas. As suggested in the previous paragraph these notions have their origins in disparate academic disciplines. In the following sections it is intended to provide an overview of some of these key concepts and contributions from the relevant literatures. Such a sketch will help to place the case studies reported and discussed in the remaining chapters in some theoretical context. Admittedly, the selection of material covered in the following sections may seem arbitrary or incomplete to some readers. However, the following groups of notions and subject areas seem most apposite to the concerns of this book: decisions and flexibility; incrementalism; and technology policy and project organization.

## Decisions and Flexibility

The first concern of the book is to improve our understanding of decision-making in uncertain situations and to contribute to the enhancement of decision-making in practice. Having said this we need to be mindful of some issues pertaining to the study of decisions and decision-making. Firstly, it is quite possible that 'decision' gets in the way of understanding decision-making (Mintzberg and Waters, 1990). The point is made that researchers tend to look for episodes of decision-making, often at the 'top' of an organization and in so doing miss the subtlety of decision-making as an ongoing process typically shaped by a variety of interests at various levels of the organization (or outside it). In addition whilst Pettigrew (1990) considers research on organizational decision-making to be 'theoretically and empirically additive' a problematic issue concerns the assumption that 'decision' equates to intentional commitment with action to follow. On this view implementation is the end stage of a linear process, which follows problem definition, search, analysis and choice. Research on decision processes in practice observes its 'recursiveness' (Sharfman and Dean, 1997), its iterative nature (Quinn, 1980) and the significance of context and process (Pettigrew, 1991). Treating decision-making as a recursive and iterative process draws attention to the cycling back and forth that decision-makers make between stages of a non-linear process. Studies of incrementalism have demonstrated the non-linear nature of decision-making in practice, and are reviewed in the next section of this chapter.

One way to approach the subtleties of the relationship between content, process and the context of decision-making is to try to analyze 'nondecision-making' as well as to commitments and action which represent the traces of decision-making that are more likely to be recorded, or recordable. As connected with the work of Bachrach and Baratz (1962) this concept draws attention to the process by which the mobilization of bias results in some options being kept off the decision-making agenda and by which the influence of certain actors is undermined. This is a notion to which the following chapters will return, as the discussion of the development of large-scale technology projects proceeds.

The key contributions on these issues over the past fifty years have offered theoretical analysis and critique of the rationalist conception of decision-making. It has become the conventional wisdom to acknowledge the limits of rationality, our own bounded rationality and the politics of decision-making. However, from time to time we see major decisions, most notably in the area of technology policy that seem to rely upon the thinking of the rational planner. On one view of this world, objectives are clear and constant, utilities transparently calculated, the problem confronting decision-makers (or more usually the individual 'decision-maker') is well-specified and incontrovertible. Data analysis can be 'thrown at' this problem to identify and to evaluate options leading to the selection of the optimum solution. Such an approach to decision-making may rely upon confident forecasts (of demand, costs and revenues) upon which sophisticated infrastructure will be installed. On another view the comprehensiveness of the analysis is relaxed. Instead of applying data to uncover the range of options open to the decision-maker, analysis is collected in support of one preferred option, to justify its selection (Carley, 1980). Whatever version of the model is employed this type of 'synoptic' rationality rests upon the assumption that

> provided the right formula has been followed, the chooser can have confidence that whatever might happen in the future, there will never be a need to recognize [that] that original choice was erroneous and in need of revision, hence [there is] no point in searching for mistakes (Collingridge, 1992: 5).

The making of decisions in this manner contravenes what is known about the ordinary way in which human beings incorporate learning through low-cost trial and error into future decisions and actions. Fundamental to this concept of the decision-making process is the view that we all make mistakes and that these not only occur but, moreover, are unavoidable. The efficient detection and remedy of errors to allow a new course of action to be pursued may be frustrated by the 'irreversibility' (Douglas and Wildavsky, 1982, with regard to the control of risky technology) and also the 'indivisibility' of decisions (Schulman, 1975). To the extent that large-scale technology ventures can be said to have enjoyed success whilst breaching the rules concerning the adoption of approaches enabling efficient trial and error learning, a degree of comfort may be offered to policy-makers and managers operating in this manner. In contrast, the failure of such grand technology projects allows approaches valuing low-cost trial and error experimentation to be retained. Such approaches refer to need for flexible decision-making, discussion of which follows.

*Flexibility*

In general notions of flexibility refer to the capacity of decision-makers to modify strategies, policies or operations in the light of new circumstances or information, and at low cost. Genus (1995) considers flexible decision-making in terms of the degree of freedom of manoeuvre decision-makers have. The distinction has been made between the content of flexible decisions (referring to the extent to which alternative decision options are kept open) and the flexibility of decision processes (Sharfman and Dean, 1997: 192). Flexible decision processes are described as those that open up the decision process to new possibilities and ideas and away from stereotyped responses and routines. The distinction has also been made between information processing and ideological perspectives of flexibility (Sharfman and Dean 1997). In essence, research on flexible adaptation, which may be identified with the information processing perspective, focuses on the constraints to flexibility connected to decision-makers' mental models and cognitive structures. The impact of these cognitive barriers biases the thinking of decision-makers and hence the range of actions they take. On the other hand, ideological factors linked to corporate culture or societal values shape decision-making in a number of areas including the awareness and definition of problems. In addition, the definition and legitimacy of objectives as well as the merits of alternative options may be skewed by core and shared beliefs and other normative influences. The distinction between information processing and ideological perspectives of flexibility may be considered in the context of the tension between competing explanations of the escalation of commitment to failing decisions (c.f. Drummond, 1999). Whereas a social-psychological explanation would focus on biased interpretations and ignorance of available information, along the lines suggested above (Staw and Ross, 1987), decision dilemma theorists look for factors that prevent better information being obtained about the risks involved (Bowen, 1987). These explanations of continued or escalating commitment to a course of action represent another line of discussion in the chapters below, regarding the sense of mission driving high profile projects and the barriers to managing them rationally. A further consideration concerns the constraints on future action associated with the specialized nature of assets required for large-scale technology investments. Here, Harrigan's (1985) view of what she calls strategic flexibility refers to the barriers to exit from declining industries presented by a firm's current investments. Such assets may be difficult to dispose of in a market short of potential buyers and so cause decision-makers to be 'locked into' previously taken decisions. This aspect of industry structure, she argues, may be exacerbated when the assets in question are dedicated to a specific use, or cannot easily be redeployed.

## Incrementalism

The concept of incrementalism is most closely associated with the work of Charles Lindblom (1959; 1968; 1977; 1979; 1990; with Woodhouse, 1993). Lindblom makes the point that, understood in terms of the content and scale of decision-making, organizations rarely make 'root' changes to the status quo. The demands on information, our inability to compute from perfect information the optimum decision even if with the necessary data, and our preference to turn our backs on 'ills' suggests another model of decision-making which Lindblom calls the alternative the 'branch' or 'incremental' method. Here, only a limited number of courses of action marginally different from the status quo are considered as potential options for change. An important aspect of Lindblom's view of incrementalism is that of seriality. In other words, decision-makers attack problems in an on-going way, such that incrementalism is a dynamic concept, and not a justification for conservatism or inertia. Further, it is an idea that prizes trial-and-error forms of learning, since the necessary experimentation that will bring forth innovation is done in a relatively small-scale way. In addition to the issue of the scale of decision-making, a second facet of incrementalism may be identified which relates to the structure and processes for decision-making. This embraces questions of the role of participation in and analysis for decision-making. Key is the emphasis on the politics of decision-making. Lindblom and Woodhouse (1993) argue that though imperfect, 'intelligent democracy' can attend to many of the difficulties of complex social problems with which analysis cannot cope (for a summary of limits to analysis see Table 1.1 below). Those interested in better social problem-solving should therefore focus on trying to understand what factors contribute to the effectiveness of intelligent democracy and which may facilitate its improvement.

**Table 1.1 Limits of Analysis**

a) poor quality/usability of policy research and data
b) fallibility:
- decision-making without political interaction can only take place where information and reasoning are sufficient bases on which to persuade parties
- information available is usually either of overwhelming or insufficient quantity or biased
- actors do not believe in the infallibility of information or experts

c) analysis cannot resolve conflicts of values
- e.g. what is the public interest?

d) time and cost
- in complex or urgent situations decisions cannot wait until 'all the facts are in'; decision-makers draw on whatever is available

e) problem 'formulation'
- problems to which analysis may be directed are not 'given'; their priority ordering is not set either - these entail moral questions and issues of values and judgement. 'The settlement requires politics more than analysis'.

*Source*: Lindblom and Woodhouse, 1993, chapter 2, pp. 20-22.

The factors that contribute to effective, intelligent democracy should not be confused with what seems to be the accepted wisdom concerning the success of democratic systems over totalitarian ones. This centres upon the responsiveness of policy-makers to popular control, either via the electoral system or freedom of speech, the press and so on. However, free societies are not necessarily capable of organizing to solve problems well and some democracies choose regimes that overthrow democracy. Instead, it has been observed that good social problem solving might be seen to rest upon certain key processes that are currently not used enough, with the effect that fundamental social problems persist over decades. Where policy does work it is when these processes are employed to good effect albeit in an unwitting manner. Overall, these 'strategies' allow such problems to become 'far more manageable than could be achieved via analysis alone' (Lindblom and Woodhouse, 1993: 24).

Briefly, the processes alluded to above include: partisanship; search for agreement; various forms of 'strategic' analysis; and the fragmentation of analysis among partisans. One of the defining features of the incremental approach is the recognition of the self-interest of partisans who pursue their own policy goals and have their own definitions of an issue. This recognition helps to side-step the old chestnut of how to make rational choices based on the best, unbiased analysis. Rather than to rely on analysis to facilitate an objective definition of a policy issue or its solution, partisanship may be thought of as 'substituting politics for analysis' (Lindblom and Woodhouse, 1993: 26).

The role of analysis in complex problem-solving is to facilitate the political interactions of partisan interest groups. The intelligence of the policy process is raised to the extent that partisans use data to persuade other protagonists: on the basis of reason; in ways which seek out what Quinn (1980) termed 'zones of indifference'; or by appeal to the likely preferences of other parties. These processes may be considered more 'intelligent' processes of winning over rival viewpoints than the use of non-rational or irrational means represented by propaganda campaigns, vetoes, or bribes which do not require the persuasion of others of the merits of the option in question *per se*. The agreement or understanding that occurs as a result of these political interactions represents accommodations that a 'working majority' of partisans make regarding future actions. It is not necessary for there to be agreement on the definition of a problem or the facts of the matter. Indeed there may continue to be substantial differences in the formulations that various groups have of an issue and the options they favour for its resolution.

The essence of the incremental approach to the content of decision-making is that actions be modest rather than radical. The prescribed method for the analysis of decisions is for decision-makers to confine their deliberations to options varying only marginally from the status quo and the remedy of 'egregious ills' (Morone and Woodhouse, 1986). The view that decision-makers do and ought to engage with policy issues in a 'serial' rather than a comprehensive manner attracts criticism for tinkering with fundamental problems (most notably from Arrow, 1964; Dror, 1964; and Etzioni, 1967). The incrementalist's retort to this suggestion is to challenge the critic to find instances where a 'once-and-for-all' approach has been demonstrably more effective than an incremental one in coping with difficult policy issues. On the contrary, one of the advantages of such an approach is that it enables efficient trial and error. The concept of intelligent trial and error thus builds upon an understanding of decision-making as an iterative process. As policy-makers revisit fundamental problems (such as poor housing or poverty) they are able to test out new policies in a small-scale way, thus avoiding the risks of the bold leap in the dark. With the latter grand strategy approach trial and error comes dear: risk-takers might argue that fortune favours the brave, incrementalists prefer strategies that enable ongoing improvement through the implementation of modest innovations and the avoidance of high costs.

The social fragmentation of analysis constitutes another important process for enhancing the intelligence of democracy. To some extent this strategy has already been reviewed in this section, since it concerns and underpins the political interactions of self-interested partisan groups. What might be usefully added here is to point to the possibility that partisan groups

> will neglect important considerations outside the scope of their immediate pursuits...Rather than relying on any one set of analysts or partisans to attend to every issue in superhuman fashion, different people become watchdogs for different social problems and needs...For any given problem...various groups will attend to somewhat different aspects of the issue, producing different kinds of information as their contributions to political interaction. For cleanup of hazardous waste dumps...community groups may do informal door-to-door surveys of health symptoms, local governments may test water samples, a state environmental agency may conduct research on the business responsible for dumping the waste, and the federal Environmental Protection Agency may study chemical compounds at the site and evaluate whether the site belongs on the Superfund list for federally funded cleanup (Lindblom and Woodhouse, 1993: 30).

On this account success in policy is facilitated, though not guaranteed, by a diversity of agencies each shedding light on some part of a problem, leading to the recognition of a wider range of issues. However, the fragmentation of analysis may be undermined if such social 'probing' is 'impaired', to use Lindblom's (1990: Chapter 5) terms. Probing is related to inquiry. Some limits on our capacity for rational inquiry are well known and relate to the extent to which we are boundedly rational. Cognitive limits on human information processing have already been mentioned in this chapter; it is the social and political dimensions of impaired probing that are of most relevance to this section. Socially or politically impaired probing means that would-be participants in decision-making will not be able to play their role within the process of fragmented analysis. Impaired probing may occur when responsibility for or influence over decision-making is concentrated in the hands of a few central actors rather than dispersed. More subtly, it can occur if educational institutions produce citizens who are unable or unwilling to think critically. Overall, such processes work against the generation and fair competition of ideas needed to make fragmented analysis a realistic proposition. Remedies for impaired probing include the practice of greater scepticism about policy on the part of professionals or experts, who also need to become more open to being challenged. More broadly, there is need to improve the thinking and understanding of 'ordinary citizens' on key issues. This means tackling the top-down nature by which people obtain much of their information on a topic, including their reliance upon certain media, which tend to reproduce dominant views and norms (Lindblom and Woodhouse, 1993).

Some questions arising from this brief review of the incremental approach may now be posed, which are central to the work of the book. First, are decisions that vary greatly from the status quo (i.e. those that are not incremental) prone to fail, as the incremental position contends? Secondly, are any difficulties associated with large-scale decisions explicable by reference to the concept of trial and error? Thirdly, is success or failure necessarily or even usually related to the particular forms of political interaction and fragmented analysis identified by Lindblom and his colleagues? Are big mistakes (for example in technology development) the product of centralized processes of decision-making? Do such processes marginalize the more modest options that are available? Such questions have been addressed with regard to previous research on large-scale technology, and inform the case studies presented in Part II of this book. The work of Lindblom has been central to the work of researchers having an interest in flexible decision-making and the control of large-scale or risky technology. This and other related developments are discussed in the following section.

## Construction and Control of Large-scale Technology

The present section addresses a matter that has been the source of much debate over the past few decades – how to tackle the dilemma associated with the promotion and control of large-scale technologies. This dilemma is revealed in the extent to which such technology simultaneously affords both opportunities to secure high economic and other benefits but also risks the perpetration of heavy costs or harm. Two broad approaches to dealing with this dilemma are represented by research in the general area of the social construction of technology and studies of the management of major projects (most notably Morris and Hough, 1987). Within the former one might identify research on the social control of technology (Collingridge, 1980; 1983; 1992; Morone and Woodhouse, 1986; 1989) and studies of constructive technology assessment (CTA, as associated with the work of Rip and colleagues, in Rip, Misa, and Schot, 1995a and 1995b; Rip and Schot, 1997). A brief outline of some key concepts in the social construction literature prefaces the discussion.

A number of concepts related to the SCOT (social construction of technology) approach have been applied to examine the adoption and implementation of inflexible technology and are of relevance to the cases presented in Part II of the book. These include the notions of 'momentum' and 'reverse salients' (Hughes, 1983) and 'interpretative flexibility' (Pinch and Bijker, 1987). Technological momentum is a term that may be applied to connote how the integration of physical artifacts, capital and scientific and administrative capabilities enable the evolution of a large-scale technological system. Of particular interest, here, is the application of momentum to convey the process by which technological systems appear to have a life of their own, but in the sense of the maturing of technology development rather than in any deterministic sense of technology acting autonomously. Technological momentum thus refers to the 'collective pressures of multiple system components, from internal corporate bureaucracies through technical artifacts to managerial and financial institutions, which develop as the system moves through the evolutionary pattern' (Hamlett, 1991).

Where the notion of momentum relates to the aspects of a developing technological system that collectively contribute to its establishment, the concept of reverse salients refers to the potential unevenness of this momentum. In particular, reverse salients is a notion that conveys how certain components of an evolving technological system may be 'out of phase' with other components, so as to limit the potential of the developing system. In the study of research and development of offshore wave energy in the UK, the link between reverse salients and uneven momentum was demonstrated in the decision to direct research to towards a gigantic 2000 MW wave station when the basic scientific questions were far from being resolved (see Chapter 4, below). Finally, interpretative flexibility refers to the idea that there are different possible options for designing an artifact but also to the idea that different meanings and roles that are accorded to technology by various parties who interpret it variously (Pinch and Bijker, 1987). The first of these is a feature of all of the case studies in the book. On the second, rather than to regurgitate Pinch and Bijker's (1987) now ubiquitous tale of the bicycle, one may cite Mort's (1995) identification of interpretative flexibility with respect to plans for Trident submarine building in the UK in the 1980s. On one hand construction of the submarine could be presented as a means for ensuring future employment for years to come; on the other hand another way of interpreting the plans was to view over-dependence on one technology as a potential threat to future employment. Appeal to notions such as interpretative flexibility may illuminate the study of the uncertainty of technology development. Some apposite questions for a new 'natural history' of technology development analyzed in this way might include: analysis of 'how interpretative flexibility is reduced in practice', how 'uncertainty [is] converted into risk' in the economic analysis of innovations, or how 'participants judge whether they are attempting incremental or radical innovation' (Mackenzie, 1992: 39).

Some further relevant ideas emanate from Callon's (1987; 1986; 1992) work depicting the dynamics of techno-economic and actor networks, by invoking concepts of translation, irreversibilization and convergence. Translation refers to the process by which: a) one actor defines others, their interests or strategies; and b) the media in which such relations are inscribed such as meetings, public announcements, texts, money, knowledge and skills, or machinery (1992: 81-2). The successful realization of a techno-economic network may to some extent depend upon the nature of this translation process, and this in turn will be subject to processes of irreversibilization and convergence discussed below. To take the notion of irreversibilization first, Callon states this as being 'synonymous with normalization' (1992: 91) where normalization occurs with the standardization of the actors' behaviour and norms, and of the means and rules of coordination between them. With respect to translation, irreversibility refers to the 'impossibility...of returning to a situation in which it was only one possible option amongst others'. Callon stresses that a translation 'more or less strongly' predetermines future translations and the identity of the actors. However the process of irreversibilization is relational in nature, one 'whose outcome depends on the actors in play" and, like the 'durability' and 'robustness' of the translation, 'one which can only be measured in the fray' (1992: 89-90). These are not, Callon argues, properties and processes that one can measure independently. As for the process of convergence within a techno-economic network, this is connected to the degree to which alignment and coordination occurs, where these relate to the extent that the actors in it work together 'in a common enterprise, without their status as actors being under constant challenge'. Convergence also refers to the ease with which the various activities of the actors are consonant with each other, despite their heterogeneity, so that 'any actor belonging to the network, whatever their position (researcher, engineer, salesperson, user, etc.) can at any time identify and mobilize all the network's skills without having to get involved in costly adaptations, translation or decoding' (1992: 87). Fundamentally, and unlike traditional sociology (or political science) actors may be animate or inanimate. An actor network comprises as series of 'heterogeneous elements', which have been connected for a period of time (Callon, 1987). The possibility of technological transformation depends on the extent to which different elements in an actor network 'resist' development, whether this originates in user expectations, the objectives of industrialists, or some aspect of the underlying science or technology (1987: 96). Both irreversibilization and convergence can increase or decrease; any apparent stabilization conferred by these processes may be temporary and/or localized. Where Pinch and Bijker are concerned to 'preserve the social environment' (Bijker et al, 1987: 13), which shapes technology, Callon, like Hughes (1983) sees a 'seamless web between the social and the technical'; the sociological, the techno-scientific and economic evaluations are interwoven (1987: 84). Moreover engineers are sociologists in the analyses, evaluations and designs they make. Following these and the other actors within actor-networks provides the means for investigating technology as a tool for sociological analysis (Callon, 1987). Though there are differences between Callon's actor networks view, Pinch and Bijker's social shaping and Hughes' notion of large-scale technology systems it is what they share that is of consequence to the chapters below. Between them they draw our attention to opening up both 'black boxes' of technology and society. They encourage the researcher to examine closely the relationship between the content of technology and values within society. Also, they lend a certain fluidity to the analysis of the evolution of technology, taking in interpretive aspects of evaluation and design, and the possibility of the 'failure' of technology development. Such thinking is influential on this book. As yet there has been little dialogue between constructivist and control approaches to studying technology development. This volume represents an effort to further the debate, hinged on recent developments in the sub-field of constructive technology assessment.

*Social Control of Technology and the Emergence of CTA*

The work of Collingridge and colleagues has asserted a link between non-incremental decision-making, inflexible technology and the poverty of control over and performance of technologies under scrutiny. This condition has been borne out in cases analyzing the nature and performance of technology from the system building of high-rise housing in the UK, to the development of nuclear power in the UK, US and France and to the technology for irrigation in various developing countries. The nature of the policy process in cases such as these is peculiar. The studies assert a link between centralization of decision-making and the selection of 'big decisions' regarding the scale of technical options selected. Those options are defined as inflexible technologies. Inflexibility in this regard is a notion that is connected with the issue of non-incrementality in the sense that technological options that cannot be taken incrementally are likely to exhibit certain characteristics when implemented. In particular, four factors are found to characterize an inflexible technology:

a) long lead time;
b) high capital intensity;
c) large unit size;
d) dependence upon specialized infrastructure.

Non-incremental decisions regarding technology are, in Schulman's (1975) terms, likely to be 'indivisible'. The sunk costs and other commitments that are made to get the project off the ground feed the rationale that such decisions are not subsequently reversible. Essentially, inflexible technologies are typically associated with 'big projects' that only very large organizations - public and private - are able to fund and realize technically. The danger is of eye-catching, glamorous but costly technological adventures being pursued, with an 'unholy alliance' between business and government militating against less ostentatious technical alternatives, which might be forwarded by those political actors who are marginalized (or missing) from the policy process.

The social control of technology viewpoint has been attacked for its preoccupation with the independent effects of technology upon social action and for conceptualizing technology as hardware (Johnston, 1985), the hallmark of technological determinism. Using different terms, Grint and Woolgar (1997) prefer to label as 'technicist' research that aims to analyze conjoined 'technical' and 'social' aspects of technology development, but retains the flavour of technology acting autonomously. The criticism has also been made that the social control view represents a naïve, rationalist and 'overly modernist' view of our ability to control technology development, and to clearly define the nature of 'good' versus 'bad' technology (Coombs, 1995). Whatever the line of attack or the preferred language, the problem is that such studies potentially neglect networks, values and meanings, which shape perceptions of the need for new technologies, evaluations of their performance, or technical design (c.f. the introductory essay in MacKenzie and Wacjman, 1985). The condition is exacerbated by the researcher's own reference to the need to 'control' technology, as if 'it' were running amok 'causing' irreparable damage to society (c.f. Collingridge's book title, 'The Social Control of Technology', also Langdon Winner's 'Autonomous Technology'). However, it is recalled that the motivation for doing this research on large-scale technology was as much to illuminate processes of decision- and policy-making as it was concerned with technology *per se* (Collingridge, 1989). Decision-making and policy-making (noting Lowi's (1970) point about the micro-social focus of research on the former and the macro-social, governmental emphasis of studies of the latter) are undeniably social activities and processes. Not infrequently such processes will be stimulated by or influence material considerations, including those concerning hardware, finance and so on. In this regard, then, what is required is to identify and exemplify conjunctions between the human, non-human, and trans-human actors referred to by Hughes and by Callon. In this book this means analyzing the significance of what is labelled large-scale or inflexible technology to different parties and what this means for the predispositions they have and the courses of action that they take. This includes looking at the legitimation and commitment to entrenched 'big' infrastructure projects before and after the decision to go ahead with them has been taken. To some degree, then, this book is concerned with the socio-political organization of decision-making. It thus connects with what Hill (1988) saw as the political hegemonies and wider social and cultural factors that help promote or inhibit technology development, and with which technology is intimately enmeshed.

For Rip, Misa and Schot (1995a) the problem is expressed in society's affinity with new technology and its inability to build a constructive relationship with technology. Like Collingridge, the focus of attention is on how to resolve the tension between the gains to be won from technological innovation for governments, corporations and society at large whilst controlling the potentially severe impacts of such development. To manage technology better within society requires a shift away from the traditional two-track approach to technology policy, whereby governments have set up separate agencies in a bid to balance the promotion and control/regulation of new, often controversial technologies. Whilst such a two-track approach once served a useful purpose, for example in splitting responsibilities for promotion and control between agencies where these may have been centralized within one department, its effectiveness has diminished over time. One of the principal sources of this demise has been cited as a 'growing crisis of credibility' regarding government, large corporations and science (Wynne, 1996). Another concerns the nature of oppositional politics, as observed in debates over nuclear power and now biotechnology. The trenchant nature of these debates results, it is claimed, in plenty of criticism but essentially makes for intractability rather than resolution of the issues as the process of claim and counter-claim persists. Moreover, new techniques of technology and risk assessment that have been proposed as remedies for the deficiencies of the two-track approach

> have hardly been effective...in solving the underlying problem. While the aim of these approaches is to provide early warning and offer a perspective on future impacts of technologies, they serve primarily as after the after-the-fact gatekeepers (Rip, Misa and Schot, 1995a: 2).

What is proposed instead of the two-track approach is called 'constructive technology assessment'. This involves the building of bridges between promotion and control activities to resolve the problems outlined above. This bridge-building reflects what Rip and his colleagues see as a recently recognized and 'essential' aspect of contemporary society – the co-production of technology. In short, the way in which impacts of technology are considered and managed is the joint responsibility of promoters and opposition groups; they share responsibility for the co-production of impacts rather than being the representatives of the division of labour entailed in the two-track approach. In this way, it is argued, challenges to technology development can come before rather than after-the-fact. The generation of processes that can enable 'societal learning about how to co-produce technology and its impacts, and how to achieve desirable outcomes' are central to the establishment of the constructive technology assessment approach (Rip, Misa and Schot, 1995a: 3).

For Rip and his colleagues CTA has its origins in the broadening of technology assessment in the US, Denmark and Netherlands in the early 1980s such that the new approach 'recognized the aspects, as well as the actors, that were involved and taken into account in the design and development of new technology' (1995a: 6). Developments during the 1980s saw increasing attention (for example in Denmark and Netherlands) to the issue of societal learning, as distinct from merely attempting to improve the public understanding of science and technology. The measures taken to improve social learning included widening public involvement in the development of information technology and biotechnology, for example, in the Danish case by means of 'consensus conferences'. Rip notes the reference made to CTA by the OECD as a more subtle approach to technology assessment that can minimize social conflicts and mismatches wrong investments.

A distinction is made between CTA and the approach taken by incrementalists such as Collingridge regarding the proper focus and conceptualization of technology assessment and control. In particular, it is argued that Collingridge has a misconceived view of the process by which technology is shaped. Though they recognize that there are problems associated with controlling technology, linked to the belated discovery of the impacts of development, and to the difficulty of making changes once entrenchment has ensued, Rip and his associates are critical of the argument for flexible technology. They assert that

> entrenchment is necessary to implement a technology. To pursue full flexibility will make it impossible to develop any technology at all. Making technology inflexible is part of the domestication and appropriation of technology which involves control (1995a: 8).

Further, they suggest that Collingridge mistakenly assumes that a "yes/no" decision is involved at some definite point the process of selection, when the policy process is more accurately observed as subject to ongoing analysis. As Rip, Misa and Schot (1995a: 8) put it

> Technical change is shot through with assessments by various actors. In fact, there are continual attempts to exert some influence, and it is out of the interplay of actors and their assessments that technology is shaped.

Ultimately, the point is made that rather than to see technology as 'out of control', a view linked implicitly with the position taken by Collingridge, the problem of technology development ought to be seen in terms of the need to change the 'present dynamics of control', so that better paths towards entrenchment are 'actively sought and shaped' (Rip et al, 1995a). As subsequent chapters show, it also warrants some inspection of the contested nature of decisions to proceed with or to withdraw commitment from large-scale technology, and the nature of debates that take place regarding the design or performance of embryonic technology.

Proponents of CTA offer illustrations of the possibilities of bringing about socially durable technology. They do also point to the difficulties of changing the course of entrenched technology paths through CTA for the betterment of society. For instance, Jorgensen and Karnoe describe how, initially, the development of modern Danish wind energy technology broke with the conventional wisdom concerning energy generation and distribution. There are two salient points to be made. First, efficient generation took place in small units – in this case, with one exception, many small (20-50 kilowatt) wind turbines formed the basis of development. Specific State subsidies for the purchase of wind turbines are cited as measures employed to stimulate the market and to protect the embryonic industry as it began to be established. Second, the role of 'grass roots' developers of technology is noted, facilitated by 'wind meetings' to bring together disparate would-be entrepreneurs, 'DIY' builders and the alternative energy movement. This is contrasted with the conventional view that the best locus for developing new energy technology lies with scientific and technical research and development based in large utility companies. Against this, it is questioned whether some of the social envisioning underpinning activities until the 1990s has been undone as the market has become increasingly concentrated and the power utilities have sought to regain their dominance over R&D programmes (Jorgensen and Karnoe, 1995).

To quote a second example of CTA, Steward considers the persistence of chemical 'trajectories' in the process of flour milling in the UK baking industry from the 1870s to the middle of the twentieth century. He compares this with the substitution of physical for chemical technologies in dairy products preservation at an earlier point within the same period, from the 1920s. In both areas the risks to public health of the existing chemical processes were uncertain. In both bread baking and dairy preservation a commercially viable physical alternative to the chemical process was available. In flour milling the physical option was represented by the use of an aeration process rather than Aegene; in the dairy sector the physical processes available included refrigeration or pasteurization whereas the extant chemical process was to use boron preservatives. The essential difference between the two cases is cast in terms of the facilitation of a constructive view of technology assessment within dairy preservation and the constraints upon such an approach within baking. In the former case a more constructive approach was permitted by the emergence of a prominent professional public health constituency having support from some sections of the industry. In baking, what prevented such an approach was the supremacy over policy of a cogently organized sectional interest, namely the flour millers, who also had the advantage of being technically very adept

> The flour millers established a strong technological basis to their industry in which cereal chemistry occupied the center stage. Although only one section of an industry, in which farmers and bakers were also important, the flour millers exercised a hegemonic role by exploiting a notion of technological progressiveness and the national interest...Their commitment to the use of chemical bleachers and improvers was established early on and consistently and forcefully maintained (Steward, 1995:120).

The central role played by the flour millers in making policy was bolstered by their close connection with the governmental departments that had had responsibility for maintaining bread and flour supply for the nation during the Second World War. By contrast, Steward notes the atomized nature of competition within the dairy industry, and the lack of a cogent lobby to act on its behalf. This, along with the advocacy of the certain key individuals, organizations (such as the National Institute for Research into Dairying, the National Clean Milk Society the British Dairy Farmers Association) and private firms (Express Dairies and Aylesbury Dairy company) contributed to the emergence of physical preservation processes. Paradoxically, however, fragmentation within the sector also helped to maintain the use of chemical processes. In addition, the dairy case study reveals a move away from risk assessment, based on the toxicity measurements of different chemical treatment techniques towards a consideration of the relative merits of alternative processes. Hence over time comparisons began to be made more in terms of a choice between rival physical and chemical processes and a working principle concerning the speed with which potentially, if not definitively, harmful chemical processes could be eradicated. This represented an important shift in thinking about the problem. Until the 1920s the issues were debated on the basis of analyses of the risks associated with the application of small amounts of boron preservative, the harm that this might cause to the public health and whether the experimental research was conclusive. From that time on the scientific findings were treated with greater caution and accorded less authority (Steward, 1995).

Wynne addresses some aspects of social learning and controversy linked to technology assessment and risk that have implications for the conceptualization and conduct of CTA. For example, there are various concepts of social learning embraced by contributors to the topic and these are explicated with more or less precision or clarity. To illustrate the range of these approaches to social learning, Wynne distinguishes between those contributors who see social learning in terms of the improvement of information flows within or among policy-making institutions and those associated with critical theory for whom controversy is tantamount to improving social learning. Between these ends of the spectrum lies a central position occupied by those who conceive of social learning as the mutual processes of interaction between policy-making entities and those involved in implementation or enforcement activities. This notion of social learning as relational is significant to the extent that

> there is more to play for in the 'social assessment of science and technology' than is apparent from prevailing languages of impacts. The latter imply falsely, that models of the human subject, social values and identities are not expressed and imposed in the developing technology itself...The reflexive version of social learning would involve the systematic exposure, investigation and debate of the implicit social models and assumptions that structure 'factual' analyses of technologies, impacts and risks. Although these social commitments influence debates about technologies and risks, their hidden role often leads to the degeneration of debate, rather than its enlargement (Wynne, 1995: 31).

CTA as represented by Rip and colleagues represents something more of an umbrella term or broad church than a clearly articulated concept, or closely defined methodology. The underlying social visions implicated in the various conceptions of the CTA framework range from stringent prescriptions for the better organization of society 'so that...technology will behave in accordance with established risk assessments', to gentler hypothesizing about the prospects for changing society in this or that direction. What is missing, Wynne argues, is explication of the social values underpinning the particular model in question. This is to 'the detriment of more robust learning, and perhaps of more socially robust technologies' (1995:32). Some further matters arising from the above are of relevance to this volume. First, the explication of the social visions, values and models to which Wynne refers may take different forms. He, for example, characterizes the approach taken by Callon, for example, as focused upon 'technological empires in the making' whereas his own studies have 'involved the retrospective analysis of technologies which have run into trouble'. The latter are considered to address the unconscious social visions of actors that condition perceptions of risk and technical assessments, compared with the former type of study wherein the conscious and deliberate nature of such visions is to the fore. With respect to the case studies discussed in the chapters below it is a combination of these latter approaches that is to be found; representing as they do historical accounts of technology development, and interrogation of the stated and latent visions that may be said to have been influential on the progress of the projects concerned. Secondly, a fundamental objection to CTA is that, by emphasizing the anticipation of impacts, positive or negative, the approach 'misses the central point'. Attending to the identification of the impacts is insufficient, albeit that their definition is made with greater sensitivity to context and 'sociological richness'. Rather, it is argued that an explication of what values are reflected in or reproduced by different technical options is necessary. Such values and interests are 'indeterminate and emergent' in character, as is technology development, and are shaped in the process of debate about development. Ultimately, this 'collective values-learning...may be the most critical and difficult element of the whole challenge of more constructive social shaping of technology' (Wynne, 1995:33). Uncovering such debate-values-choice processes is central, here.

From the disciplinary vantage-point of economics constructive technology assessment proceeds from the recognition of the unequal sharing of costs and benefits from technology development, and hence the need for an approach 'focusing on the broad societal integration of technology as well as the adaptation of technology to societies' needs' (Soete, 1995: 45). Avenues for realizing a 'dynamic' economic perspective for constructive technology assessment involve the abandonment of the search for 'socially optimal' technology and institutions, traditionally the substance of economists' assessment of long-term impacts and externalities of technical options. Such searches for optimality will tend to ignore the emergent, evolutionary character of technology and society. Instead, a dynamic approach requires experimentation, social learning and constructive feedback that can guide the future development of technology.

The dynamic approach, it is suggested, will address 'the costs of experimentation, as well as irreversibilities that may be introduced because of the real-life character of experimentation, [and that] must be balanced against the potential advantages [of the technology]' (Soete, 1995: 46). Soete considers the role of technology assessment institutions and other actors as being to facilitate and to engage in these processes of experimentation and learning and feedback. For Callon, CTA may merely represent a 'utopian dream' if it fails to address properly the matter of whether and how all of the actors involved in development get their voices heard at the table. Similarly, the implementation of CTA would be the poorer if it did not answer questions of how to keep open alternative technical options, or how to avoid irreversibilities that emerge due to lack of prior support for alternatives (Callon, 1995). Suggestions for improving the conduct of constructive technology assessment in practice are presented in the epilogue to Rip, Misa and Schot's edited volume on CTA (Rip et al, 1995b) and a recent paper by Schot and Rip (1997) on the topic. Notably, they include the practice of 'creative incrementalism' (Rip et al, 1995b: 350). The measures cited are stated as follows:

1. use sociotechnical foresight and prospective mapping tools (rather than trend extrapolation forecasting methods);
2. use forceful visions of the future and forceful demonstrations and pilots; such 'technology forcing' may be a good way to elicit debate and learning;
3. stimulate interactive demand articulation through 'strategic niche management';
4. recognize the decentralized nature of technology development processes in the modulation of technical change (it is in this regard that creative incrementalism is specifically advocated);
5. facilitate social learning through processes to align the actors, creation of new actors or nodes, and the specification of loci for social learning.

It will be instructive to compare these proposals for the future advancement of CTA with those of the more thoroughgoing treatment of incrementalism applied to technology development in the case studies below, and in previous work by Collingridge and colleagues. In the last chapter of the book it will be possible to explore the areas of overlap between the two approaches to indicate the potential complementarity of CTA and social control frameworks. The complementarity of the two approaches may be informed advantageously by contributions deriving from the economics and sociology of technology development discussed in preceding paragraphs.

*Project Management*

In project management terms the book adopts a strategic perspective of technology development, an extension of the approach advocated by Morris and Hough in their studies of the management of major projects (Morris and Hough, 1987; Morris, 1997). This seeks to locate a concern with various activities and techniques across the project life cycle (such as design, construction, installation, scheduling or contracting) within the context of the economics of projects and the financial or other objectives of relevant parties. Here though the 'strategic' view is more thoroughgoing. The life of a project does not end with commissioning, it is as enduring as the technology systems under review are, referring to the longevity of related artifacts, developers, finance, users, opponents, plans and the connections between them. Being strategic in orientation also implies that aspects of organizational and wider culture values are significant for understanding the objectives and management of projects, somewhat broader in remit than is usually the case in the project management literature. However, from Morris and Hough's (1987) analysis of eight major projects and an exhaustive survey of literature on the topic, myriad 'key' success factors are cited, relevant to life cycle or scheduling issues in project management.

At the risk of over-simplification these key factors involve the need for clarity of project definition but the avoidance of premature or over-commitment. The importance of maintaining a philosophy valuing flexible design is another factor in the management of major projects clearly of relevance to the ideas of this book, as is Morris and Hough's advice that design should be frozen once it is agreed by the parties and after adequate testing has been carried out. Here, the extent to which client-contractor relationships are antagonistic and reflective of a lack of mutuality detrimental to development also reinforces the lessons of previous work in project and strategic management. Some helpful insights on this issue comes from the work of Stinchcombe (Stinchcombe and Heimer, 1985). This seeks to identify aspects of contracting and coordination that smooth or exacerbate the management of complex undertakings. As this book will show asset specific infrastructure may well be organized through inter-firm contracts and subcontracts rather than internalized with firm 'hierarchies' as predicted by Williamson (1975). Instead, what becomes of significance is the extent to which various coordinating and control devices, such as routines for specifying who has authority to make design changes, incentive systems, or dispute resolution operate effectively. To the extent that they do, contracting parties may be able to work cooperatively and the project governed efficiently. There is a connection between these ideas and concepts such as alignment to be found in the SCOT approach. So, for example, Morris and Hough themselves cite the importance of teamwork, *inter alia*, to the success or failure of a number of projects, including the Channel Tunnel between 1960 and 1975, the advanced passenger train and the Thames barrier. At the same time the strategic management and strategic networks literatures have drawn attention to the significance of trust and mutual objectives to success in joint ventures and inter-firm collaboration (Jarillo, 1988; Kanter, 1989; and Thorelli, 1986). A further issue of relevance to the following chapters is the warning to avoid 'concurrency'. This occurs where the urgency of a project's schedule, combined with technical uncertainty, leads to the simultaneous and problematic conduct of design and construction (as demonstrated in Morris and Hough's Fulmar North Sea oil field case study and experience with first generation AGR nuclear power stations).

## Layout of the Book

The principal concern of this book is to generate insights into the socio-political construction and difficulties of managing large-scale technological projects. It adopts a multi-disciplinary approach to the task (c.f. Shapira and Berndt, 1997), based on an application of concepts of flexible and incremental decision-making, project management and the social construction of technology. Incremental decisions regarding technology projects are proposed to be more flexible than non-incremental decisions that are indivisible, lumpy and irreversible. Moreover, the general orientation of incrementalism predisposes decision-makers to value variety and 'reversibilization' rather than the uniqueness and 'there is no alternative' thinking associated with grand projects (Lampel et al, 1996). Fundamental to incrementalism is the view that all decisions are open to error, which can be guarded against by the adoption of relatively small-scale decisions and on-going trial and error learning. This learning best occurs through a process of socially fragmented analysis and debate. Overall, such an approach affords some protection to decision-makers in the likely event of changed circumstances or new information rendering selected options out of date or mistaken. It therefore contrasts with the taking of non-incremental 'leaps in the dark', which may be considered to be an altogether more hazardous and vulnerable exercise.

In the following chapters the book seeks: to evaluate the inflexibility and non-incrementality of technology projects; to analyze aspects of the policy, selection or design process in order to assess the extent to which certain actors and options may have been marginalized; and to identify implications for effective collaboration of relations between the principal actors in the project. The ramifications of these technological, policy and organizational issues for the performance of the different cases are analyzed. Overall, the research offers case studies with which to examine the prescriptive claims of the incremental approach to decision-making. They do not by any means constitute a representative sample for the purposes of generalization but add to the body of material producing insights into the merits of incrementalism and the management of grand projects. The following propositions guide the analysis:

1. inflexible technology projects will be unusually difficult to develop and will incur severe financial, technical, environmental or human costs;
2. the development of inflexible technologies involves centralized choice whereby legitimate stakeholders are excluded from the policy process and a few dominant organizations are able to shift the financial risks of development onto the public purse;
3. there are more flexible technological alternatives than the selected option, which may be developed in a decentralized manner.

With regard to the first proposition, the four indicators mentioned above may be employed to characterize an inflexible technology: high capital intensity; large unit size; long lead time and heavy dependence on specialized infrastructure. Investigating the second proposition proceeds by addressing the role and influence of various governmental and corporate and other actors on the choice, funding and design of the technology concerned. The central questions here concern the extent of any financial exposure of the public purse, various administrative and contractual arrangements and the implications these have for the effective management and social robustness of technical developments. Finally, the third hypothesis is based on the consideration that there is no inevitability about the choice or design of a technology. Other more flexible alternatives exist which represent small-scale, incremental options and which may be implemented according to the rules of incrementalism, i.e. in a decentralized way.

The analysis is applied to the three case studies that make up Part II: exploration and development of the first generation of UK oil and gas fields; the construction of the Channel Tunnel; and UK policy towards wave power in the 1970s and 1980s. Each presents a challenge to the ideas expressed in the book regarding incremental decision-making and provides some insight into various aspects of technology development and project management. For example, the North Sea oil case study constitutes a severe challenge to incrementalism. Nobody doubts the technical achievement involved in the opening up of a pioneering oil province in an extremely inhospitable environment. Similarly, the financial and economic benefits associated with development and production activities seem beyond question. This seems to be an example of a successful large-scale technology project contravening the incrementalist prescription. However if one delves beneath the surface there is another story to be told. Telling this story is the work of Chapter 2. Chapter 3 presents the Channel Tunnel case study. This would seem less taxing a challenge for incrementalism than the North Sea oil case; after all the financial difficulties of the project and Eurotunnel are well known. Nevertheless, there remain some questions regarding how the costs should be balanced against the engineering achievements associated with infrastructure that should be available for use for many years to come, and what an incremental approach would do differently. Also where the North Sea oil case is concerned with relations between actors at the policy level (between large oil companies and Department of Energy), in the Channel Tunnel case study inter-firm, client-contractor, aspects of project management come to the fore. The third case study is of UK policy towards wave power in the 1970s and 1980s. Central to this case study are the predispositions of certain key actors that affected the determination of the required size of prototypes and load factors assumed for research, development and demonstration purposes (linked to decision-making over future central funding for wave power in the UK). The wave power case study is presented in Chapter 4. The two remaining chapters of the book (Chapters 5 and 6) form Part III. Here, the findings from the case studies are drawn together, first in terms of the implications of the cases for the propositions outlined above, and secondly in terms of their bearing on the wider literatures that inform this short book. Part II, comprising these case studies, now follows.

## References

Arrow, K. (1964), 'Review of: A Strategy of Decision: Policy Evaluation as a Social Process', *Political Science Quarterly*, vol. 79, pp. 584-588.

Bachrach, P. and Baratz, M. (1962), 'Two Faces of Power', *American Political Science Review*, vol. 56, pp. 947-952.

Bijker, W.E., Hughes, T.P. and Pinch, T.J. (1987), 'Introduction', in W.E. Bijker, T.P. Hughes, and T.J. Pinch, (eds.), *The Social Construction of Technological Systems: New Directions in the Sociology and History of Technology*, MIT Press, Cambridge, Mass., pp. 11-15.

Bowen, M.G. (1987), 'The Escalation Phenomenon Reconsidered: Decision Dilemma or Decision Errors?', *Academy of Management Review*, vol. 12, pp. 52-66.

Callon, M. (1986), 'The Sociology of an Actor-Network: the Case of the Electric Vehicle, in M. Callon, J. Law, and A. Rip (eds.), *Mapping the Dynamics of Science and Technology*, Macmillan, London.

Callon, M. (1987), 'Society in the Making: the Study of Technology as a Tool for Sociological Analysis', in W.E. Bijker, T.P. Hughes, and T.J. Pinch, (eds.), *The Social Construction of Technological Systems: New Directions in the Sociology and History of Technology*, MIT Press, Cambridge, Mass., pp. 83-103.

Callon, M. (1992), 'The Dynamics of Techno-economic Networks', in R. Coombs, P. Saviotti and V. Walsh (eds.), *Technological Change and Company Strategies*, Academic Press, London, pp. 72-102.

Carley, M. (1980), *Rational Techniques in Policy Analysis*, Heinemann Educational Books, London.

Collingridge, D. (1980), *The Social Control of Technology*, Frances Pinter, London.

Collingridge, D. (1983), *Technology in the Policy Process: Controlling Nuclear Power*, Frances Pinter, London.

Collingridge, D. (1989), *Personal correspondence.*

Collingridge, D. (1992), *The Management of Scale*, Routledge, London.

Coombs, R. (1995), 'Firm Strategies and Technical Choices', in A. Rip, T.J. Misa, and J. Schot, *Managing Technology in Society: the Approach of Constructive Technology Assessment*, Pinter, London, pp. 331-345.

Douglas, M. and Wildavsky, A. (1982), *Risk and Culture: an Essay on the Selection of Environmental Dangers*, University of California Press, Los Angeles, California.

Dror, Y. (1964), 'Muddling Through – Science or Inertia', *Public Administration Review*, vol. 24, pp. 153-157.

Drummond, H. (1999), 'Analysis and Intuition in Technological Choice: the Lessons of Taurus', *International Journal of Technology Management*, vol. 17, pp. 459-466.

Etzioni, A. (1967), 'Mixed Scaninng: A 'Third' Approach in Decision-making', *Public Administration*, vol. 27, pp. 385-392.

Genus, A. (1995), *Flexible Strategic Management*, Chapman and Hall, London.

Grint, K. and Woolgar, S. (1997), *The Machine at Work: Technology, Work and Organization*, Polity, London.

Hamlett, P. (1991), 'The Political Construction of Technology', *personal memorandum*, December.

Harrigan, K.R. (1985), *Strategic Flexibility*, Lexington, Lexington, Mass.

Hill, S. (1988), *The Tragedy of Technology: Human Liberation Versus Domination in the Late Twentieth Century*, Pluto, London.

Hughes, T. (1983), *Networks of Power: Electrification in Western Society: 1880-1930*, John Hopkins University Press, Baltimore, Maryland.

Hughes, T. (1987), 'The Evolution of Large-scale Technological Systems', in W.E. Bijker, T.P. Hughes, and T.J. Pinch, (eds.), *The Social Construction of Technological Systems: New Directions in the Sociology and History of Technology*, MIT Press, Cambridge, Mass., pp. 50-82.

Jarillo, J.C. (1988), 'On Strategic Networks', *Strategic Management Journal*, vol. 9, pp. 31-41.

Johnston, R. (1985), 'The Social Character of Technology: Reply to Collingridge', Social Studies of Science, vol. 15, pp. 381-383.

Jorgensen, U. and Karnoe, P. (1995) 'The Danish Wind-Turbine Story: Technical Solutions to Political Visions', in A. Rip, T.J. Misa, and J. Schot, *Managing Technology in Society: the Approach of Constructive Technology Assessment*, Pinter, London, pp. 57-81.

Kanter, R.M. (1989), *When Giants Learn to Dance*, Unwin, London.

Lampel, J., Miller, R., and Floricel, S. (1996), 'Information Assymetries and Technological Innovation in Large Engineering Construction Projects', *R&D Management*, vol. 26, pp. 357-369.

Lindblom, C.E. (1959), 'The Science of Muddling Through', *Public Administration Review*, vol. 19, pp. 79-88.

Lindblom, C.E. (1968), *The Policy-making Process*, Prentice-Hall, New Jersey.

Lindblom, C.E. (1977), *Politics and Markets*, Basic Books, New York.

Lindblom, C.E. (1979), 'Still Muddling Not Yet Through', *Public Administration Review*, vol. 39, pp. 517-527.

Lindblom, C.E. (1989, 4 October), *Personal correspondence*.

Lindblom, C.E. (1990), *Inquiry and Change*, Yale University Press, New Haven.

Lindblom, C.E. and Woodhouse, E.J. (1993), *The Policy Making Process* (3rd edition), Prentice-Hall, New Jersey.

Lowi, T. (1970), 'Decision-making vs. Policy-making: Toward An Antidote for Technocracy', Public Administration Review, vol. 30, pp. 314-325.

MacKenzie, D. (1992), 'Economic and Sociological Explanation of Technical Change', in R. Coombs, Saviotti, P. and Walsh, V., *Technological Change and Company Strategies*, Academic Press, London, pp. 25-48.

MacKenzie, D. and Wacjman, J. (eds.) (1985), *The Social Shaping of Technology*, Open University, Buckingham.

Mintzberg, H. and Waters, J. (1990), 'Does Decision Get in the Way?', *Organization Studies*, vol. 11, pp. 1-6.

Morone, J. and Woodhouse, E.J. (1986), *Averting Catastrophe: Strategies for Regulating Risky Technologies*, University of California Press, Berkeley, CA.

Morone, J. and Woodhouse, E.J. (1989), *The Demise of Nuclear Energy, Lessons for Democratic Control of Technology*, Yale University Press, New Haven, Connecticut.

Morris, P.W.G. and Hough, G.H. (1987), The Anatomy of Major Projects, *A Study of the Reality of Project Management*, John Wiley, Chichester.

Mort, M. (1995), 'Constructing Trident, Reinforcing the Network, Technology Analysis and Strategic Management, vol. 7, pp. 307-313.

National Audit Office (2000), *Ministry of Defence Major Projects Report 1999*, Stationery Office, London.

Pettigrew, A. (1990), 'Studying Strategic Choice and Strategic Change: A Comment on Mintzberg and Waters: Does Decision Get in the Way?', *Organization Studies*, vol. 1, pp. 6-11.

Pettigrew, A. and Whipp, R. (1991), *Managing Change for Competitive Success*, Blackwell, Oxford.

Pinch, T.J. and Bijker, W.E. (1987), 'The Social Construction of Facts and Artifacts: Or How the Sociology of Science and the Sociology of Technology Might Benefit Each Other', in W.E. Bijker, T.P. Hughes, and T.J. Pinch, (eds.), *The Social Construction of Technological Systems: New Directions in the Sociology and History of Technology*, MIT Press, Cambridge, Mass., pp. 17-50.

Quinn, J.B. (1980), *Strategies for Change: Logical Incrementalism*, Irwin, Homewood, Ill.

Rip, A., Misa, T.J. and Schot, J. (1995a), 'Constructive Technology Assessment: A New Paradigm for Managing Technology in Society', in A. Rip, T.J. Misa, and J. Schot, *Managing Technology in Society: the Approach of Constructive Technology Assessment*, Pinter, London, pp. 1-12.

Rip, A., Misa, T.J. and Schot, J. (1995b), 'Epilogue', in A. Rip, T.J. Misa, and J. Schot, *Managing Technology in Society: the Approach of Constructive Technology Assessment*, Pinter, London, pp. 331-345.

Schulman, P.R. (1975), 'Non-incremental Policy Making: Notes Toward an Alternative Paradigm', *American Political Science Review*, vol. 69, pp. 1354-1370.

Shapira, Z. and Berndt, D.J. (1997), 'Managing Grand-scale Construction Projects: A Risk-taking Perspective, *Research in Organizational Behaviour*, vol. 19, pp. 303-360.

Sharfman, M. and Dean, J.W. (1997), 'Flexibility in Strategic Decision-making: Informational and Ideological Perspectives', *Journal of Management Studies*, vol. 34, pp. 191-216.

Soete, L. (1995), 'Constructive Technology Assessment: an Economic Perspective', in Rip, A., T.J. Misa and J. Schot, *Managing Technology in Society: the Approach of Constructive Technology Assessment*, Pinter, London, pp. 37-51.

Staw, B.M. and Ross, J. (1987), 'Behaviour in Escalation Situations: Antecedents, Prototypes and solutions', in L.L. Cummings and B.M. Staw, (eds.), *Research in Organization Behaviour*, JAI Press, London, pp. 39-78.

Steward, F. (1995), 'Risk Analysis and Rival Technical Trajectories: Consumer Safety in Bread and Butter', in A. Rip, T.J. Misa and J. Schot, *Managing Technology in Society: the Approach of Constructive Technology Assessment*, Pinter, London, pp. 111-135.

Stinchcombe, A.L. and Heimer, C. A. (1985), *Organization Theory and Project Management*, Norwegian University Press, Oslo.

Thorelli, H. (1986), 'Networks: Between Markets and Hierarchies', *Strategic Management Journal*, vol. 7, pp. 37-51.

Williamson, O.E. (1975), *Markets and Hierarchies: Analysis and Anti-trust Implications*, Free Press, New York.

Wynne, B. (1995), 'Technology Assessment and Reflexive Social Learning: Observations From the Risk Field', in A. Rip, T.J. Misa and J. Schot, *Managing Technology in Society: the Approach of Constructive Technology Assessment*, Pinter, London, 1995, pp. 19-36.

Wynne, B. (1996) 'Misunderstood Misunderstandings: Social Identities and Public Uptake of Science', in A. Irwin, and B. Wynne, (eds.), *Misunderstanding Science? The Public Reconstruction of Science and Technology*, Cambridge University Press, Cambridge, pp. 19-46.

# PART II
# CASE STUDIES

# 2 UK North Sea Oil

## Introduction

The UK North Sea oil case study offers some rich insights for the theoretical analysis and practical management of large-scale technology projects. In this chapter the story of early experience of exploration and production in the province is related. It encompasses the period between 1965 and 1990, during which the first generation of oil and gas fields in the UK sector of the North Sea underwent development and during which the greatest technical and organizational challenges were confronted. In common with the other case studies in this book this chapter presents an analysis of decision processes relevant to North Sea activities, connecting aspects of oilfield technology, performance evaluation, industry-government relations and social choice. Central to the analysis are connections between the scale of decisions taken, the processes through which these have emerged and the difficulties faced by policy-makers and corporate strategists in a pioneering province such as the North Sea. Further, with the vast contribution made by North Sea oil and gas revenues to the UK Treasury over the last twenty-five years, it seems that here is a story of undeniable success. To the extent that this is so the prescriptions of incrementalism are contradicted. The following sections indicate that such success owes a debt to serendipity and that there are a number of lessons for policy and management to be taken from the case study. A little background to the case is required in order to place events in some context. This is provided in the next section, after which follow sections on the inflexibility and non-incrementality of North Sea oil decision-making, the centralization of decision processes regarding North Sea exploration and licensing policy, for example, and the implications of all of this for performance. A concluding section draws together the various strands of the chapter.

## The North Sea - A Pioneering Oil Province

In 1998 prices, total investment expenditure on North Sea activities for the period 1965-1988 was £73 billion. Indeed, for much of the period reviewed it represented over one-fifth of total UK industrial investment (Department of Energy, 1989). Overall, in 1999 terms, investment in the region has been estimated at about £160 billion since the mid-1960s, and the UK Treasury has benefited from a similar amount in taxation paid from oil production activities since the mid-1970s (UKOOA, 1999). By any stretch of the imagination this constitutes a very hefty commitment; it would have been so without unforeseen increases in cost and delays in development. Not surprisingly, at the time of the development of the earliest and largest fields, investment in the North Sea was described as the riskiest and most expensive offshore venture in the history of the oil industry (Scott, 1972).

For most new projects, a critical stage is reached with the sinking of the exploration and development costs. Without this spending, production cannot be realized. However, the nature and magnitude of the prior investment needed to achieve this is such that decision-makers find it difficult to modify policy in the light of changed circumstances or advances in knowledge. This is a condition that Collingridge and James (1989a; 1989b) have identified in previous work, in other areas of technology policy where inflexible technology projects have been pursued. Many of the technical problems of work in the North Sea have arisen from the combined efforts of deeper than average waters for an offshore area and extremely adverse weather conditions. These environmental factors have made necessary the development of extremely robust equipment and larger structures than previously employed in offshore work. This can be observed at various stages of the evolution of North Sea oil projects.

One shortcoming of early seismic data, for example, was lack of penetration, especially through the Zechstein salt layer, limiting interpretations of the underlying Permian Sandstone to gross structural descriptions (Fier, 1972). As surveys tended only to establish that certain geological conditions were present, costly exploratory drilling was made all the more necessary. Such drilling was almost always carried out using highly specialized semi-submersible rigs. These float on the surface with a large substructure reducing the impact of waves of between 60-70 feet and winds of up to 100 mph and more, while operating in water depths of 200-400 feet (Fetters, 1971). In contrast, the Gulf of Mexico the main source of available offshore development experience in the early-1970s offered more benign conditions for exploration and development. Despite this, only eleven floating rigs were in operation in 1972, when to satisfy the lease commitments on Fourth Round concessions alone entailed the drilling of some 300 exploratory wells. With only a few companies owning their own rigs, this scarcity was to be reflected in charter rates. In 1972, estimates of exploratory drilling costs (i.e. rig plus services) were of the order of $350,000 per day (in 1998 terms), (Scott, 1972) falling by 1976 to between $55-85,000 per day (1998 terms) (Trimble, 1976). The southern area of the North Sea, in comparison, bore drilling costs of around $180,000 per day in 1972 (1998 terms), jack-up rigs being more feasible here than in the central and northern North Sea waters where oil activities were concentrated. Further, the cost of the new rigs under construction at the time was estimated at approximately $180 million each (1998 terms) (Scott, 1972). There were further problems to be confronted in the exploratory drilling phase. Briefly, these included shortages of qualified personnel and the 25% downtime that supply operations suffered as a result of bad weather. In terms of personnel, operators and contractors alike were to find that the lack of engineers and divers, and so on, presented a source of cost escalation, which few could have foreseen (Scott, 1972). Improvements in supply operations necessitated new vessel designs aimed at increasing unloading speed and safety and continuing research into the effect of the weather on operations and equipment (Kennedy, 1974).

Turning to the development stage of fields deemed to be commercial following exploration and appraisal, similar signs of inflexibility may be observed. For Shell UK, for instance, three factors were to seriously constrain their approach to field development. These were: the technological barriers which had to be overcome; the lack of detailed information available at the time that major development decisions were being taken; and bound up with the foregoing, the need to get into production as early as possible after the commitment of 'big money' (Heaney, 1973). Platform techniques, for example, have been the subject of constant revision in the battle to surmount the difficulties arising from the environment of the northern North Sea, in particular. Here, it seems as if the companies seriously underestimated the severity of the conditions and the time it would take to build and install the facilities required (Trimble, 1976). These platforms have had to incorporate new features relevant to supply and platform space, sit in record water depths and weigh in the region of thirty thousand tons, without equipment, making them the largest ever built. They have also necessitated the development of special growing docks for their construction and new construction techniques for their installation (Craven-Walker, 1973). This has involved the evaluation of completely new materials and design concepts, including concrete structures secured in place by gravity.

There has also had to be the design and construction of prefabricated packaged units on the necessary scale for drilling and production facilities, for power generation, for pollution control and for living and recreational needs. Units such as these would have to last for over 20 years or more, with minimum maintenance. The fact that, in general, platforms were subject to at least year-long delays in delivery and installation, should therefore be of little surprise. Platforms consume a vast proportion of total development expenditure and often up to 60% of the initial capital expenditure required to realize any production at all. The combination of size and cost, especially, foreclosed the option of smaller scale, more gradual learning about North Sea platform technology, which in any case would have clashed with prevailing oil policy. So, the policy makers considered that they simply had to have faith in their investments once made, since remedial action would achieve little in savings and possibly would only have incurred greater costs.

The Piper field provides a good example of this type of problem. Here, the field was developed using a single steel platform costing nearly £850 million (in 1998 terms) and occupying a central role in that area's oil and gas transportation. The wreckage of the platform, on 6 July 1988, resulted in the 167 deaths, and loss of production, with a £3 billion loss of gross cashflow to the economy (i.e. revenue before taxes but after the deduction of capital and operating costs). In addition, the costs of redevelopment have been estimated at £400 million, compared with original pre-production development expenditure of £555 million (money of the day). Further, the transportation of production from other fields using the Flotta system has been disrupted (County NatWest Woodmac, 1989).

Another aspect of field development, exhibiting similar qualities to the above, concerned the transportation of the oil ashore, whether by pipeline or marine terminals. Thus, in addition to severe weather conditions, the pipeliner was faced with problems of servicing and supplying the pipeline operation. Even small diameter pipe could be unwieldy and the transfer of joints of pipe from a supply barge to the pipelaying vessel represented a hazardous operation. Consequently, it became very difficult to keep crews and equipment services. Other problems peculiar to the North Sea included submerged wrecks and mines, fishing trawlers trailing their nets and trawls along the sea floor and marine traffic coordination, in what is a very busy area. Moreover, in the earlier years, land-pipelining techniques were extended to marine pipelining requirements. Hence valves, manifolds, separators and gaskets were applied directly, frequently without modification to the task at hand (Lynch, 1965). As work has progressed farther north, so pipelines have become ever more difficult to install. In 1972, Shell estimated that a 150-mile line in 450 feet of water would require three summers to install, north of the 62nd parallel. Work would be possible for only three months of the year, so that only 50 miles per year could be laid (Scott, 1972). The cost of such activity has been enormous, with the Brent field's share of the Brent pipeline system (which serves several fields) alone amounting to approximately £400 million at 1989 prices (County NatWest Woodmac, 1989). Costs have been exacerbated by the price of line pipe doubling during 1973 and 1974 (Trimble, 1976).

## Analyzing Inflexibility

With reference to the factors cited above, first generation North Sea oil projects may be said to be inflexible. This point has been at the heart of this chapter and may be highlighted in a more rigorous manner. In particular, it may be possible to outline the cost of North Sea infrastructure in comparison with existing technology in less hostile areas of exploration, the capital intensity of North Sea projects and the lead time necessary to reach production start-up.

The cost of specialized infrastructure has been indicated, above, by the disparity between hire costs for various types of drilling vessels used in differing offshore environments. The demands on capital of North Sea exploration and development infrastructure in the oil-bearing central and northern areas, may be further illustrated as follows. For example, in 1974 money, drilling ships were estimated to cost £6-8,000 per day to hire, jack-ups £10-12000 per day and semi-submersibles £15-25,000 per day (Mackay, 1975). At one point during that year, the charter rate for the semi-submersibles needed to drill the deepest and roughest waters increased to over £40,000 per day. Remembering that well-drilling typically took two or three months, this adds up to quite a considerable cost. Flotation collars were developed specially in order to facilitate the construction of jacket structure platforms. Yet due to the stresses involved each one could only be used twice and cost over £140 million (in 1998 prices). In addition, the cost of the special coating required to protect deeply laid North Sea pipelines in the first wave of field development was over £200,000 per mile. Notably, the cost of laying pipe at that time was roughly between £2-4 million per mile (1998 terms). Considering that several North Sea pipelines, certainly the major ones, are about a hundred miles in length shows the great expense entailed in the employment of this type of infrastructure. Table 2.1 and Table 2.2 provide support for the claims that North Sea oil projects are inflexible and non-incremental by virtue of their long lead times and their capital intensity, respectively. Lead time is given for various fields and is measured in two ways: the time in months elapsing between the date of the discovery of a field and production start-up; and the time in months elapsing between the granting of development consent for the field (its 'Annex B') and production start-up. The latter period represents the development stage where capital expenditure is greatest. Capital intensity is given as the ratio of capital expenditure to total expenditure, which is expressed as a percentage. In Table 2.2, the relevant estimates for capital, operating and total expenditure are given as they apply to each barrel of oil produced from the fields in question, future production being estimated.

Considering Tables 2.1 and 2.2, it is clear that long lead times and high capital intensity are features common to North Sea oil projects. The very first North Sea fields to be developed (including the largest ones) had commenced development by the end of 1973 when oil prices were, in real terms, at a comparatively low level (under $20/bbl in 1998 terms). Moreover, Forties field, the single largest on a solely oil reserve basis (Brent is larger if gas reserves are included), had by this time received about half its pre-production expenditure. This figure of £1.3 billion (1998 prices) represents 27% of estimated lifetime capital expenditure and 24% of total field expenditure (both figures discounted at 15%). Now, suppose that oil prices had remained at a steady but much lower level from 1973 onwards rather than the OPEC-induced quadrupling of price that actually occurred. What consequences could there have been for such an investment? The first point to make is that a field of such dimensions as Forties (over 2.5 billion barrels of recoverable reserves) would be unlikely to lose money, despite the amount of capital required for its development. This is so even if relatively high discount rates are used, since the economies of scale available to a field as comparatively simply structured as Forties permit very low per unit costs. However, the real problem to be addressed is that of maintaining flexibility and encouraging economically efficient methods of development, rather than obtaining benefits without reference to the costs of so doing. If hypothetically low prices during the mid-1970s had the same effect as they actually did a decade later, then it may reasonably be assumed that lower oil prices would have heightened government and industry awareness of the need to develop more cost-effective technology. Presumably, this awareness would have translated into developments that were smaller, with shorter lead times and, as in the case with fields served platforms, lower capital intensity and infrastructure requirements. The role of high oil prices in creating a false perception concerning the success of early North Sea technology is considered below.

**Table 2.1 Lead time for various North Sea oil fields (months)**

| | A<br>Date of<br>Discovery | B<br>Annex B<br>Received * | C<br>Production<br>Start-up | A-C | B-C |
|---|---|---|---|---|---|
| Alwyn N. | Oct. 1975 | Oct. 1982 | Nov. 1987 | 145 | 61 |
| Argyll | Sept. 1971 | Feb. 1973 | June 1975 | 45 | 28 |
| Auk | Feb. 1971 | Feb. 1972 | Dec. 1975 | 58 | 46 |
| BerylA | Sept. 1972 | July 1973 | June 1976 | 45 | 35 |
| Brent | July 1971 | Aug. 1972 | Nov. 1976 | 64 | 51 |
| Buchan | Aug. 1974 | Mar. 1978 | May 1981 | 81 | 38 |
| Clyde | June 1978 | Dec. 1982 | Mar. 1987 | 105 | 51 |
| Cormorant S | Sept. 1972 | May 1974 | Dec. 1979 | 87 | 67 |
| Duncan | Jan. 1981 | Oct. 1983 | Nov. 1983 | 34 | 01 |
| Dunlin | July 1973 | May 1974 | Aug. 1978 | 61 | 51 |
| Forties | Nov. 1970 | Dec. 1971 | Sept. 1975 | 58 | 45 |
| Heather | Dec. 1973 | Aug. 1974 | Oct. 1978 | 58 | 50 |
| Magnus | July 1974 | Dec. 1978 | Aug. 1983 | 109 | 56 |
| Maureen | Feb. 1973 | Jan. 1978 | Sept. 1983 | 127 | 68 |
| Montrose | Dec. 1969 | Mar. 1974 | June 1976 | 78 | 27 |
| Ninian | April 1974 | June 1974 | Dec. 1978 | 56 | 54 |
| Piper | Jan. 1973 | April 1973 | Dec. 1976 | 47 | 44 |
| Statfjord UK | April 1974 | n/a | Nov. 1979 | 67 | n/a |
| Thistle | July 1973 | July 1974 | Feb. 1978 | 55 | 43 |

* Formal Annex B approvals were not granted prior to the Petroleum and Submarines (Pipelines) Act of 1975. Where fields were developed before the enactment of this legislation, the dates quoted in column B refer to the time when informal Department of Energy consent was given or field development work was initiated. For such fields, the precise timing of informal Annex B consent can be vague and consequently lead times have been estimated.

*Sources*: Various editions of the Department of Energy, *Development of the Oil and Gas Resources of the United Kingdom* (HMSO, London), and County NatWest Woodmac's North Sea Service, National Westminster Investment Bank Group, London.

## Public Policy and Project Management Issues

### *Licensing and Taxation Regimes*

Following the Geneva Convention, the Continental Shelf Act of 1964 extended British sovereignty to the continental shelf and, subsequently, laid down terms for companies wishing to exploit oil and gas discoveries in the Petroleum (Production) Regulations. The Minister of Power, as the post was then known, decided to establish a discretionary licensing system, as opposed to asking for cash bids from interested companies. Licences were to be of two types: exploration licences allowing for only preliminary geological survey work; and production licences necessary for any large scale drilling activity. Under such a system, which has remained the principal one for allocating licences since 1964, companies submit their proposed work programmes to what is now the Department of Energy. The first phase of North Sea development was characterized by a policy encouraging rapid development, with many of the best prospects being offered early on, often in batches, as part of large licensing rounds.

Indeed, in more definitive terms, a continuing aim of all British governments during the 1960s and 1970s has been stated (Department of Energy, 1978) as being

**Table 2.2 Capital intensity of various North Sea oil fields (1989 values discounted at 15% p.a.)**

| | capex/bbl | opex/bbl | total cost/bbl | capital intensity% |
|---|---|---|---|---|
| Alwyn North | 4.64 | 1.09 | 5.73 | 81 |
| Argyll | 3.06 | 2.67 | 5.73 | 53 |
| Auk | 3.41 | 2.32 | 5.73 | 60 |
| Beryl (A+B) | 1.42 | 0.55 | 1.97 | 72 |
| Brent | 2.09 | 0.50 | 2.59 | 81 |
| Buchan | 5.08 | 2.06 | 7.14 | 71 |
| Clyde | 3.73 | 1.39 | 5.12 | 73 |
| Cormorant South | 3.29 | 0.72 | 4.01 | 82 |
| Duncan | 6.25 | 4.05 | 10.30 | 61 |
| Dunlin | 3.10 | 0.83 | 3.93 | 79 |
| Forties [a] | 1.27 | 0.20 | 1.47 | 86 |
| Heather | 7.40 | 1.70 | 9.10 | 81 |
| Magnus | 2.32 | 0.66 | 2.98 | 78 |
| Maureen | 5.52 | 1.30 | 6.82 | 81 |
| Montrose | 3.44 | 1.86 | 5.30 | 65 |
| Ninian | 3.49 | 0.67 | 4.16 | 84 |
| Piper [b] | 1.49 | 0.40 | 1.89 | 79 |
| Statfjord UK | 0.21 | 0.11 | 0.32 | 66 |
| Thistle | 4.74 | 1.10 | 5.84 | 81 |

*Notes*: a. Figures do not include the later incremental South-east Forties development.
b. Inclusive of redevelopment expenditure following the 1988 disaster.

*Source*: Author's calculations based on capital and operating cost data contained in the various annual editions of County NatWest Woodmac's North Sea Service.

> to achieve U.K. self-sufficiency in oil on a net basis (i.e. allowing for trade in crude oil products)...in order to realise the benefits of the tax revenues and of improved security of supply and the advantages for the balance of payments.

British government policy has been criticized down the years for being too lenient in its licensing policies, not capturing a great enough share of oil revenues and even for having a casual approach to the partition of the North Sea, in the first place (Sampson, 1988). In the first four rounds of licensing presaging the first upsurge in exploration activity, only fifteen blocks of a total of 2,654 blocks offered, were allocated by competitive bidding, rather than at the discretion of civil servants. These blocks, auctioned in 1971, fetched £37 million, although admittedly this was a time when demand was bound to be high because of the finds being made at the time. As for the other licences, initial payments were between £25-45 per square kilometre and the stipulated maximum annual fee between £290-350. Moreover, licences were for a period of forty-six years, and although one-half of each block would have to be surrendered after a six-year period, this was virtually at the companies discretion i.e. the least promising parts would be given up (Balogh, 1974).

Royalties were fixed at 12.5% of the well head value but there was no provision for the State to either influence or determine the posted price system, in order to receive full value. This was unlike the situation pertaining to North Sea gas where producers were forced to sell to a monopsonistic British Gas Council. As for taxation, corporation tax was payable, though there existed ample opportunity for companies to offset tax losses and allowances against these liabilities. Further, the companies benefited by way of capital grants and other financial assistance, particularly where investment activity in development areas was concerned. As well as the need to facilitate rapid exploitation, the Ministry of Power has explained this generosity in terms of its duty to protect the companies from harsh taxation abroad. In other words, it did not wish to set a precedent for OPEC countries in their dealings with the multinationals, in case this rebounded on the companies' ability to undertake North Sea exploration, or as ever, adversely affected the balance of payments situation (Sampson, 1988).

Some general points may now be made regarding the inflexibility of early licensing policy. First, although the early licensing rounds, especially the Fourth, certainly achieved the aim of stimulating oil company interest in exploring for oil, this was not obtained cheaply. (In any case, these companies had already appreciated the need for their own secure, independent crude supplies, after a period of rising Arab assertiveness over their principal economic asset.) Thus the non-existence of a nationalized oil company or independent oil sector combined with government ignorance of oil exploration in a way that enabled the control of the most precious assets to pass to the majors. Once the latter had begun to invest in exploration and the true worth of the North Sea became apparent, any subsequent attempts to control the pace of developments, or to enhance the State's position in the relationship would face difficulty. Moreover, decisions about the size and nature of the Fourth Round had to be taken by civil servants with little or no experience to draw upon, save that within the very companies that stood to gain from the allocation. Certainly, at that time (1971) there were few dissenting voices that received a hearing on the subject. This situation has been exacerbated in two ways, both of which demonstrate belated but increasing government awareness of the problems of managing oil. First, it was not until the Ninth Round (1984/5) that licensees were required to support research and development into new technology by UK-owned offshore suppliers. In addition, the original tax regime did not provide for a ring fence to prevent companies from offsetting profits from North Sea oil and gas activities against tax losses and allowances accruing elsewhere in their businesses. This only occurred after the Labour Government's Oil Taxation Act (1975), with the introduction of Petroleum Revenue Tax. So, in the early period of exploration, real incentives to increase the rate of technical innovation and so cut costs were notable only by their absence.

Official estimates of the government's take, reported by the Committee of Public Accounts in 1972/73, were in the range of 50-60% of any profit from North Sea operations. This was comparable to the returns estimated under the taxation provisions of the USA and Netherlands. However, Norway's share at this time was nearer to the top of a range extending from 55-80%, Nigeria's between 70-75% and that of Middle Eastern countries probably as high as 95% (Mackay and Mackay, 1975). The oft-quoted reason for accepting lower returns than those being obtained by other comparable oil producers was the need to provide an incentive to encourage rapid exploration. In the early days, especially it was feared that the international oil companies, having access to several sources of low-cost oil, might prefer to defer production of high-cost North Sea oil (Noreng, 1980). After all, British governments had no direct experience of oil production and little knowledge of the technical and commercial aspects of the oil industry. According to Noreng (1980) as a result of this inexperience and the somewhat enigmatic nature of North Sea oil potential in the early years, U.K. governments therefore had to opt for a dualistic relationship with the companies: on one hand, they were allies in order to explore and produce oil, and on the other hand, they were potential antagonists.

### *Depletion Policy*

One area revealing the nature of this collaboration between State and the oil companies concerns depletion policy, linked to a rather unhappy coincidence of views concerning the scarcity of resources on the UKCS Thus the consensus was that the North Sea was an oil province of only limited dimensions. This faulty alignment of viewpoints developed to the marginalization of those with a more optimistic view of the extent and potential of North Sea reserves and relatedly an alternative approach to the development of oil resources. In particular, this meant that the exclusion of small and medium independent oil companies and the views of certain academics, such as Peter Odell. Odell's view was that ultimately North Sea reserves would prove to be much greater than extrapolations from the geological and technical data of the early 1970s had suggested, the process of exploitation facilitating the discovery of new reserves. Thus the longevity of production allows time for the development of new technology in the areas of geology and oil recovery, so providing for the upward revaluation of reserves (Odell and Rosing, 1977; 1980). (More pointedly, Wildavksy and Tannebaum, 1981, suggest that it was in the interests of the oil companies to promote the view of scarce resources as this would work to keep up the price of oil and their revenues alike.)

Typically, the advocates of depletion controls appealed on economic grounds to the imperfections and failures of natural resource markets, which are said to encourage depletion at non-optimal rates (Robinson, 1982). For them, the proper role for governments and other regulatory authorities is thus to intervene to enforce the 'right' depletion rate, usually one less rapid than that which would be realized under an unregulated regime. Imperfections, here, can be characterized by the presence of monopolistic and oligopolistic competition featuring firms able to manipulate prices or output, or the possibility that market interest rates may be higher than the social time preference rate. (The latter refers to the rate at which society would discount the future, so indicating its preference for the consumption of resources now or for leaving them in the ground for the benefit of future generations.) Market failure primarily relates to adverse environmental effects involving production, transportation and the consumption of resources that do not fully enter into prices. Consequently, consumers in the market do not receive the correct price signals and may enjoy artificially low prices which stimulate the consumption of and hence the faster depletion of resources.

The major oil companies, on the other hand, were typical proponents of the pessimistic approach to reserve estimation. Here, estimates are based on current geological knowledge, with only fairly conservative assumptions being made about the future. Their belief is that the bulk of UKCS reserves had already been discovered, no large fields (i.e. over 500 million barrels of recoverable reserves) having been found in the 1980s. In the 1970s, the dispute saw the optimists justified in their assertion that the companies had underestimated the extent of North Sea reserves. Moreover, they had a vested interest in doing so pessimistic estimates of reserves have tended to encourage government tax concessions directed at maintaining the rate of exploration and drilling activity. Additionally, the use of scarcity as an excuse for higher than necessary oil prices, together with the desire of governments and companies alike for immediate cash flow has not created conditions conducive to cost efficiency.

The extent to which opportunity has been lost and flexibility in policy has suffered is partly revealed by the upward revaluations that have taken place with regard to some of the North Sea's fields (Department of Energy, various years). For example, the estimate for recoverable reserves for the Forties field has been upgraded on a number of occasions. Back in 1975, recoverable reserves were estimated at roughly 1800 million barrels. By April 1987, this figure had increased to 2,490 million barrels, a rise of over 72%. For the Beatrice field, the original view of its prospects was that it was barren. Hence, Shell returned to the Department of Energy part of a block that had already been discounted as oil-bearing. A decade later, new seismic data led B.P. to bid £22.5 million to license the same area. At least until the end of the 1970s, therefore, depletion policy was

> largely procedural, concerned with checking, if necessary modifying and eventually approving company output programmes for the future. No significant restraints appear to have been placed on current production except to reduce gas flaring (Robinson, 1981).

The machinery by which control over output and exploration might be exercised was under the Petroleum and Submarines Pipelines Act of 1975. The 1976 Energy Act could also be invoked. However, the considerable powers enjoyed by the Secretary of State for Energy in regulating production and development in the national interest were trimmed by the Varley Assurances (Robinson and Morgan, 1978). In particular, these set limits on the timing and the extent to which production could be cut. With the Varley Assurances promising no change to current company programmes before 1982, there was little that politicians could do to alter the pattern of production from fields that had already received development consent. Talk of depletion policy slid away from the political agenda as the 1980s progressed. To reduce output in any given year was not a vote-winner, and would only serve in any case to forego economic benefits now to the possible future benefit of another party (Robinson, 1990). The unwillingness of governments to apply output controls was manifest in the House of Commons Energy Committee decision to reject such controls in 1987 (House of Commons Energy Committee, 1987). Its reasons were that the control of production would only result in 'increased costs overall and ... less than maximum economic recovery.' Also, any such action on the part of government was considered to have an indeterminate influence on oil prices and thus could not be relied upon to help the North Sea oil companies out of their current problems, as had been suggested.

More indirect methods of controlling depletion include delaying field development and altering the frequency and extent of licensing Rounds. Of course, these could not be applied to the first generation of North Sea fields once these had gone into production but, again, during the mid-1970s where talk of energy crisis was very high on the political agenda such options gained currency. Similarly, the eventual direction of policy, as in the case of output controls appears to have been guided by considerations that have not always had much to do with the pursuit of economic efficiency. For example, both Labour and Conservative governments since the crucial Fourth Round have regulated the issue of production licences much more closely. Yet the Fifth Round of 1977 owed its timing (i.e. a five year gap since the previous batch of allocations) as much to the concurrent completion of the participation arrangements that Labour had introduced, as to the problems that the oil industry had had in digesting Fourth Round acreage. Similarly, the size of the Fifth Round was made deliberately much smaller than its predecessor, with 44 blocks on offer as compared to 436, though this may be explained in terms of the, stress and strain that had been put upon the domestic industrial equipment industry (Benn, 1980).

Labour had recognized that smaller and more regular licensing rounds might promote steadier development of the domestic oil equipment manufacturing industry, thus acting as a form of depletion control, which did not raise the problems of cut-backs. It was believed that whilst arbitrary cut-backs might affect the confidence of companies working in the North Sea, here was one way to determine how quickly remaining blocks were to be explored and to some extent adjust oil production to the perceived needs of the nation (Benn, 1980). Nevertheless, the main thrust of Labour's policies in this area must be viewed in terms of the State's various macroeconomic considerations and desire to redress the inequalities of its bargaining position vis-a-vis the large multinational oil companies.

Likewise, in the view of the Energy Committee (House of Commons Energy Committee, 1987: 4) Conservative governments after 1979 used the licensing regime in such a way as to enable the State to

> exercise control over the manner in which drilling is carried out, development programmes, the approval of operators, the provision of information about the licensees' activities, and the assignment of interests held under the licence policy since 1975, appears to have been on smoothing out the peaks and troughs of North Sea activity, the importance of depletion policy as a political issue being replaced by concern that there would be insufficient new fields developed to replete resources in the 1990s, and to maintain a steady supply of orders for the offshore industry.

The first development delays were announced in 1980 by David Howell, the then Secretary of State for Energy. His intention (as revealed in Hansard, 1980) was to delay the development of certain fields discovered after 1975 because of the Government's belief that

> on strategic and security of supply grounds it is in the national interest to prolong high levels of U.K. Continental shelf production to the end of the century.

However, the first such action taken - to delay production start-up from Clyde by two years - appears not to have been taken after any sort of careful examination of whether the long term interests of society were being fulfilled. Indeed, short-term issues seemed to have a greater bearing on the conduct of government policy, here, as they often do. In this case, with a public corporation, BNOC, being the field's operator and the conduct of monetary policy in full swing, delays in the development of Clyde may be viewed in terms of the Treasury and the Cabinet's desire to hold down the PSBR, by controlling the capital spending on the field (Robinson, 1982). The prevalence of short-term horizons may also be witnessed in the case of the Alwyn North field. Here, proposals for the development of the field were received by the Department of Energy in October 1982. Incredibly, approval was granted in fourteen days. The main factor behind such haste was the state of the order-starved offshore industry, which by now had become a major priority. Further, Alwyn North would not reach peak production until after the production hump of the mid-1980s and as such was not that important to any lingering questions concerning depletion policy for the 1980s.

*Participation*

The most controversial element of moves to ensure greater political control over oil matters, was doubtless the decision of the Labour Government to establish the British National Oil Corporation (BNOC). This was the main purpose of the Petroleum and Submarines Pipelines Act of 1975. BNOC became the main agent of majority state participation offshore, giving the government access to production on the continental shelf during periods of international supply disruption. Thus the licensing system was used to give a 51% share to BNOC of the new licences granted in the Fifth Round of 1977 and representation on all the operating committees, which plan the development of North Sea fields. Companies were expected to agree to participation terms for finds made under licences already issued.

Through the use of participation agreements for finds made under existing licensing terms, BNOC was also provided with the opportunity to purchase up to 51% of all oil produced, net of royalty. This was at a market price defined as that agreed between willing buyers and sellers, leaving the latter neither better nor worse off (Lynk, 1988). Compared to that of private companies, BNOC's position was also privileged in that it was allowed to obtain licences outside normal licensing rounds and was exempted from Petroleum Revenue Tax. (Companies, though, were able to buy back participation oil as a feedstock for their refineries.) In short, BNOC made for a potentially very powerful force in the North Sea, although the principle was adopted that the companies should be left financially no better or worse off as a result of participation.

Essentially, the creation of BNOC was intended to:

1. extend public control over oil exploration and production;
2. control North Sea sales; and
3. provide the government with alternative information and advice to that of the multinational oil companies.

It was, therefore, a major function of BNOC to facilitate the ability of the State to gain access to and to interpret oil field information. The then Secretary of State for Energy, Tony Benn (1980), saw the need for large-scale participation on, the grounds that 'first-hand experience is vital to gain the necessary expertise and information in all North Sea oil activities'. If the Labour Government were to control, rather than to regulate the oil industry, it clearly would have needed to be in possession of considerable information and expertise.

Labour's view in 1975, was that state intervention and control over the North Sea was in the public interest by definition, because it was a socialist action (Hann, 1986). The activity of the multi-nationals was a major and topical political issue, with strong popular support for the government to be seen to be taking some action in the oil sector. One of the problems associated with the setting up of BNOC, however, was what appeared to be a fundamental conflict of roles for the Corporation. BNOC was intended to operate both as a competitive oil company and, at the same time, as a partner of the private companies gathering confidential information and with an intimate relationship with the government (Hann, 1986). Such a duplication of roles was to be the source of great uncertainty and no little opposition, both party politically and from within the oil industry itself. This is quite ironic since the setting up of BNOC can be seen as an institutional response by government designed to enhance its ability to adapt to the uncertainties and vicissitudes of the world oil market of the 1970s. Nevertheless, the degree to which BNOC could deliver such assistance to government was hampered by its wide frame of reference, since for it to operate for the good of the nation would render it incapable of taking decisions purely on commercial and financial criteria.

Moreover, the companies feared loss of profits through retrospective and (possibly, in their eyes) immoral legislation, although eventually participation agreements were negotiated with all North Sea producers. Still, the threat that hung over future investment was real. After all, the Secretary of State for Energy now had been vested with very considerable powers of discretion over depletion and control over fields and BNOC was formed only about twenty years after the companies had begun to experience what, for them, would be the doubtful joys of selling their gas output to a monopsonistic British Gas. This had slowed the exploitation of British gas (Robinson, 1990).

Finally, once BNOC had established itself as a credible oil company, the rational ambitions of its top executives led it to seek financial and managerial independence. This it did by borrowing from commercial banks (an $825 million loan in 1977, for example) and by increasing multi-nationalization. Such moves lessened the opportunity for government control and intervention and added to the potential complexities of any future break-up of BNOC. The need for decision-making freedom on the part of BNOC's executive may be explained in the following ways (Hann, 1986). First, it was quite conceivable that the objectives of politicians and civil servants might clash with the long-term commercial aims of the Corporation. Second, and related to the previous point, if the government had been BNOC's only source of finance and the Corporation needed to request funds for an investment project, the money could be denied because it conflicted with any wider governmental objectives, rather than because of its commercial viability. The implication of the drive towards greater independence, therefore, was that political interference, rather than control or regulation, was, likely to continue, or maybe even increase over time, thus adding to the uncertainties of oil management.

This uncertainty and speculation continued into the first term of Mrs. Thatcher's Conservative Government, with the unveiling of plans which would dramatically alter the role of BNOC in the domestic oil sector. The situation was not helped by the fact that a government pledged to reduce state intervention and to dismantle BNOC would have to confront the complexities of its financial and administrative arrangements. Further, there was a realization on the part of the incoming administration of the value of BNOC revenue. These factors served only to encourage 'government procrastination and ambiguity with respect to BNOC' (Hann, 1986). In particular, the Energy Secretary, David Howell faced the political embarrassment of a domestic petrol shortage, in the summer of 1979, having to use BNOC as the instrument by which government would attempt to divert oil supplies while considering how best to dismantle it. Political pressure also came to bear from within the Conservative Party and the Government to use BNOC revenue for political and economic purposes. For instance, such funds could be used for helping to finance government borrowing.

Such a confusion of interests and views, in addition to other sources of opposition in Parliament and BNOC itself, made the complete dismantling of BNOC an unlikely option. Instead, various forms of restructuring and privatizing the Corporation were considered. Eventually, in 1982, after Nigel Lawson had replaced David Howell as Energy Secretary, BNOC was divided into two with Britoil taking over its exploration and production interests before being privatized and later taken over by B.P. By March 1985, the Government had announced that the remaining part of BNOC would be abolished as soon as possible, following its failure to effectively regulate the market price for participation oil. Throughout the winter of 1984/85, BNOC was once again to embarrass the Conservative Government. This time the administration was seen to be attempting to hold up the price of UK oil thus supporting OPEC's weakening price structure, in contradiction to its stance on free market principles. Also, with the spot price of Brent blend consistently below the official price, BNOC was forced to sell its oil at a loss, losing about £86 million during the six months to April 1985. The company's losses combined with the large subsidies it had been granted by Parliament (£65 million in three months from December 1984 - February 1985), plus the embarrassment of Conservative state intervention, made abolition all but inevitable. BNOC was replaced by the Governmental Oil and Pipelines Agency, which continued to trade royalty oil in kind but in the spot market, rather than through a system of official pricing (Lynk, 1988).

Once again, the importance of short-term political considerations in influencing policy, this time through the process of privatizing BNOC, has been illustrated. The privatization programme was a central part of Conservative policy and the privatization of BNOC was a symbolic expression of the Government's commitment to free enterprise. As for the role of BNOC in the North Sea 'play', this is something that has often been overstated. Fears that it would have a carried interest in the oil companies, i.e. let them pay for developments until the Corporation decided that it would enter the game, proved unfounded. Instead, as Hann (1986) states

> the dreaded participation turned out to be merely an option to buy oil for BNOC and an assurance that most of the refining be done in Britain.

### *Project Coordination and Contracting*

Some important consequences flow from the evolution of policy in the North Sea to the context and management of development projects in this province. As raised above these are associated with the influence of assumptions about the scarcity of oil and gas resources on the UK continental shelf and the domination of technical expertise by corporate organizations, compared with Department of Energy administrators. One concerns and is evident in the temporal pattern of North Sea development. A normal pattern of technical innovation is for a few pioneer, and therefore high-cost, developments to be made, which establish the basic viability of the technology. The experience of these developments is then incorporated into a second generation of developments, which will often be initiated by diverse entrants following a variety of technical approaches. As the technology diffuses, successive waves of development occur, each incorporating the experience of their predecessors and, in most cases, improving the performance of the technology.

This pattern was turned upside down in the case of North Sea oil, for a very high proportion of the total resource base was developed with pioneer technology. Hence, although the oil companies learnt a great deal from the first generation of fields, for example, in project management skills and designing for deep waters, there was no large second wave in which that experience could be incorporated for more than a decade. By this time some of the original learning was obsolete. This situation may be contrasted with the Norwegian case, where development was phased and, in particular, development of the more exposed northerly oil and gas fields was delayed until the 1980s and 1990s. One result of this was that the average cost of first generation North Sea fields was possibly higher than might have been than with a more staged development, which would have permitted greater experimentation, allowed greater transfer of learning and reduced pressure on the supply infrastructure.

The North Sea exemplifies some problems of project coordinaton, concerning contractual aspects of inter-firm relations and their implications for performance. A Department of Energy (1976) study of cost escalation noted a number of factors, which influenced the supervision and control of contractor performance (i.e. those reliant more on hierarchical coordinating devices than the legal obligations specified in contracts). Inadequate project management was reflected in project definition being stated in terms of achievement of target rates for realizing oil or gas production, rather than in terms of the control of costs. Indeed, according to the cost escalation study

> planning and control systems were directed at maintaining development timetables rather than at cost control, which was regarded as of subsidiary importance. Underestimation of the problems involved resulted in failure to establish appropriate management structures and systems, inadequate project definition prevented operators and contractors establishing adequate plans and applying effective controls.

Supervision by operators of managing agents and contractors and, indeed, the initial decision to contract out development activities, occurred against backdrop of over-optimism about the ability of agents and contractors to undertake these responsibilities. In addition, a lack of inexperienced in-house design and management staff swayed some decisions to contract out. Moreover, effecting a coordinating hierarchical element to the facilitation of information flow and good practice was a process hindered by the operators' deployment of in-house management without project management supervision experience. Spatial considerations are relevant since much of the contracting out was by, or to, companies from the US. These considerations again help to explain unfamiliarity or misunderstanding of UK design codes, engineering practices, industrial law and standard forms of contracts. Moreover, such misunderstandings contributed to delays, cost escalation and lack of trust between the parties. Finally, in terms of more specific aspects of contractual form, the type used in early North Sea developments was generally the cost reimbursement contract. The primary benefit of this was to secure the commitment of contractors who could rest assured that their costs for expenditure incurred would be reimbursed and they would still receive an agreed additional sum for overheads and profit. However, this form of contract requires effective procedures for recording and controlling costs, the poverty of which militated against cost-effective development of oil resources.

## Evaluating North Sea Oil Performance

The primary focus, here, is on the cashflows generated by selected fields before taxes but after both operating and capital costs have been met. This allows for the relative timing of these cash inflows and outflows. It should be apparent that for projects to perform successfully in financial terms, the aim must be to attain low costs of development and production, so that field performance is relatively insensitive to changes in oil price. In terms of the sample of fields considered, the study is primarily directed at the North Sea's earlier developments. Offshore oil fields which commenced development prior to the OPEC and oil equipment price explosion of 1973-74 present the best examples of inflexibility, bearing the brunt of the technical difficulties associated with the pioneering days of the province. Thus huge investments had to be made without the benefit of hindsight, in ignorance as it were. Fields that fall into this category all received development consent in 1973 or before. These fields are: Argyll, Auk, Beryl A, Brent, Forties and Piper. Another band of fields received development consent during the following year and so are also included in the sample. These are: Cormorant South, Dunlin, Heather, Montrose, Ninian, Statfjord UK and Thistle. (Care needs to be exercised in interpreting data regarding Statfjord UK as this forms only a small part of the very large Statfjord field, which the UK shares with Norway.) In addition to these 13 fields, some 'second wave' developments are considered, by way of some comparison. Those included in the sample are Alwyn North, Buchan, Clyde, Duncan, Magnus and Maureen. In all, this sample represents roughly two-thirds of total 'proven plus probably recoverable' oil reserves, and over half of the estimated maximum for 'possibly recoverable' reserves from discoveries made by the end of the period under review (Department of Energy, 1990).

Steep rises in the price of crude oil did much to improve North Sea field economics during the first part of the 1970s and again at the end of that decade. Consortia which sought and won development consent for their fields before mid-1973, submitted their proposals against a background of average nominal $ prices of less than $2, in 1970, and just over $4, three years later (County NatWest Woodmac, 1990). With the Arab-Israeli war average nominal prices, in 1974, leapt to over $11/bbl, and averaged around $14/bbl until the second oil crisis occurred, in the aftermath of the Iranian Revolution of 1979. The average nominal dollar price rose to a peak, in 1981, of over $37/bbl. The average real dollar price peaked in 1980 at over $80/bbl in today's prices. At the time of writing (July 2000) the dollar price of crude oil has risen to around $30/bbl. For the fields included in this study the impact of this on project economics is relatively low given the discount rates applied to the analysis of cash flow and the front end loading of investments made twenty-five to thirty years ago.

Fortunately for the companies operating in the British North Sea, the decline in the dollar price since 1981 has been matched by a parallel decline in the value of the pound against the dollar. This insulated the sterling price of crude oil during the first half of the 1980s, so that the peak in nominal prices happened in 1984 (at £23/bbl). The real sterling price remained steadier throughout this period than its dollar counterpart. In 1986, oil prices plummeted, at one stage, to below $9/bbl. Moreover, the dollar began to weaken against sterling, further depressing the sterling oil price to an average of over £10. More recently (except for the period covering the Gulf War), prices have returned to something like 1973 levels in real terms, despite wild fluctuations in the intervening period. (For example, at the end of 1998 Brent crude, the spot price of which provides the basis of the calculations below, dipped below $10 a barrel.)

The impact of these fluctuations in price has been to wreck any attempts to forecast price movements as an aid to investment decision-making and also to affect the performance of fields where such development decision-making has already been acted on. As far as the first wave of North Sea projects is concerned, one of the most notable components of the conventional wisdom of the 1970s was the way in which the level of oil prices was more or less viewed as a constant among the other variables in decision-making (Reid, 1987). One example of this was

Exxon's 1971 forecast that over the next decade Arabian crude prices would not exceed \$3/bbl (Reid, 1987). The rate of growth suggested by such a trend in nominal prices is roughly 4% per annum. If one considers this alongside rates of inflation more typical of the early 1970s than the oil-induced hyperinflation of the mid-1970s, this rate of growth vanishes to a decline in real price of equal proportions. Similarly, Geoffrey Chandler, a spokesman with Shell and then President of the Institute of Petroleum expressed his slightly less pessimistic view of the future of oil prices (Odell and Rosing, 1980). For Chandler, a rise in price to over \$7/bbl was required by 1980 to provide sufficient incentive for enhanced recovery and exploration in both old and new areas. This 1980 figure implies a real rate of growth in price of about 2%, if pre oil-crisis rates of inflation (averaging 8% per annum) are taken into account.

Adopting the latter view of price expectation, the scenarios developed below include one where a real growth in annual prices of 2% occurs (before exchange rate fluctuations are taken into account). Calculations for this scenario are based on the historic price of Ekofisk crude in 1972, when several UKCS fields had received development consent, or were about to do so. Inflationary effects are allowed for by converting all revenues and costs to 1998 terms and inflation is assumed to be 5% per annum from 1999 onwards. Sterling is the currency used in the calculations, historic rates being used to convert from US \$, future rates estimated at £1 = \$1.60.

For each field, the yearly cashflows generated are discounted in order to arrive at their present values and so account for the timing and magnitude of expenditure and income. (In other words, from the yearly gross revenues obtained from output sales, annual operating and capital costs are deducted and the resultant annual cashflows then discounted.) Given that North Sea oil is a national rather than private resource, it is reasonable that a discount rate be chosen which reflects this. In considering their worldwide alternative investments, companies pursuing commercial interests may well insist on rates of return of, say 25-40% for riskier than normal projects. However, governments are rarely presented with such opportunities to earn high rates of return on their investments. They also have to consider the economic, political and social consequences of their decision making much more carefully (Odell and Rosing, 1977). Bearing these factors in mind, a relatively conservative rate of 15% per annum is used for discounting purposes.

Tables 2.3 and 2.4 reveal the contrast to be found in field performance if one compares scenarios incorporating moderate price growth with ones based on actual prices. (In the latter, the same assumptions are made concerning inflation, exchange rate and so on.) It is remarkable how the economics of the early fields have been transformed by the sudden leaps in price of the 1970s. Thus once where many projects would have been loss-making or vulnerable with moderate price growth, they now become generally very profitable. Indeed, with the sort of price trends more reminiscent of the early-1970s, only two of the first-generation fields under review, Forties and Piper, would have been economically attractive. The same situation presents itself when, instead of a scenario based on growth over time, the price in real terms is held constant, say at $16/bbl (roughly £10/bbl). This is akin to holding constant the mid-1973 price (of Saudi Arabian light crude oil) as expressed in 1998 terms and is also much closer to the long-run supply price of oil (Odell, 1986).

One likely effect of the timing of the 1973/74 price increases, with regard to the field developments taking place at that time, was to heighten the desire of governments and companies to make rapid progress towards production. However the wish to take advantage of the higher prices available was to be frustrated by the contemporaneous effects of development delays arising out of equipment shortages and associated cost increases. Generally, the larger fields were insulated from the worst effects of this. By developing other constant price scenarios, it is possible to reconstruct the sensitivity of fields to changes in price, in order to gauge their ability to absorb increases in cost. The relative size of the operating firms involved is also important here, as this affects the degree to which it becomes imperative to cut cost, especially by way of technical innovation. Once again, Forties field would continue to be profitable under almost any reasonable price scenario, with the same assumptions as above. Only at a constant real price lower than £4.50/bbl (currently $7) does its net present value fall below zero. Under these circumstances, attending to cost might not assume the importance that it might do with a high unit cost, low output field. Such a project is the Argyll field and here the picture is vastly different. Whereas Forties is a field of giant proportions (2,500 million barrels of recoverable oil, by company estimates and peak production of 523,000 bbl/day), Argyll is very small (70 million bbl recoverable and peak production of 23,000 bbl/day). In fact, it was not until the 1980s that other fields of comparable size to Argyll were developed. Moreover, Argyll's operator and chief shareholder is Hamilton, an independent company unable to absorb or finance the high costs of development in the way that BP can, even allowing for a benign tax regime. Calculating the net present values for Argyll, as above, gives a break-even real constant price of roughly £11.50/bbl ($18). This is a vulnerable position, which would have been all the more precarious without the innovations that were in fact made. These have included the development of the semi-submersible platform and it is unlikely that bigger companies would have considered such a small project until more conventional alternatives had been exhausted. In the event, Argyll has enjoyed an extraordinarily high rate of return.

More recently, one finds a far greater concern with cost containment than hitherto. This applies to the bigger companies as well as the smaller ones. There are several plausible explanations for this. The maturity of North Sea development has meant that new projects are smaller in size than the giant fields of the 1970s. Greater attention to innovating cost-saving technology has therefore been warranted. In fact, most of the recent developments have been incremental add-ons to existing fields. In addition to this, the more stringent attitude of governments towards the North Sea has led to more punitive rates of taxation and greater willingness to control production levels. This served to increase corporate anxiety in the years after 1981 when prices began to fall. For example Clyde and Alwyn were the only two completely new projects on the UKCS during 1980-83. Ownership of Alwyn is shared by Total Oil Marine and Elf, state controlled French companies, while the principal participant and operator in Clyde has been first BNOC, then Britoil, after the privatization of the former. The timing of the development expenditure made by these companies has been affected by governmental considerations. One of these was a concern to flatten out the production peak of the mid-1980s and also to defer some production from the 1980s so as to prolong high levels of production until the end of the century (Howell, 1980). As well as this, such factors as the position of the offshore supplies industry and, in the case of BNOC, the level of the PSBR had to be taken into account before development consent could be granted.

These fields have been subjected to a discounted cashflow analysis similar to that performed for earlier fields (see Tables 2.3 and 2.4). Alwyn has a negative rate of return at a constant real price of £ 10/bbl and a very high break-even price of over £18/bbl ($28). Since more than 60% of its pre-production costs were incurred when prices were falling towards a real price of £11/bbl, it is not surprising that ways of cutting cost were found. Indeed, Total Oil Marine managed to achieve a £337 million saving on the original budget making total development costs £2.6 billion (1998 terms). Technical factors contributing to this were: a) the minimizing of offshore 'hook-up' by testing and commissioning each platform module onshore prior to sail-away; b) freezing of the basic design at a given point, thereby

**Table 2.3 Net present value of selected North Sea oil fields under various scenarios (1998 Prices in £ Millions discounted at 15% p.a., pre-tax basis)**

| Field | Historical Oil Prices | 2% pa Rise in Real Prices | £10/bbl ($16) Real Price |
|---|---|---|---|
| Argyll | 416 | -171 | -63 |
| Auk | 626 | -186 | -55 |
| Beryl A | 2534 | -169 | -144 |
| Brent | 4033 | -2204 | -3106 |
| Forties | 19533 | 5438 | 6047 |
| Piper | 9120 | 2373 | 2813 |
| Alwyn N. | -1373 | -1064 | -1354 |
| Buchan | 385 | -250 | -341 |
| Clyde | 7 | 209 | -23 |
| Cormorant | 252 | -1228 | -1681 |
| Duncan | 34 | -103 | -138 |
| Dunlin | 2960 | 86 | 116 |
| Heather | -23 | 763 | -804 |
| Maguus | 2270 | 1091 | 248 |
| Maureen | 626 | -85 | -529 |
| Montrose | 357 | -314 | -279 |
| Ninian | 7034 | -914 | -1383 |
| Statfjord UK | 1557 | 602 | 165 |
| Thistle | 2422 | -939 | -929 |

*Source:* Calculations are based on data from County NatWest Woodmac's North Sea service/Wood Mackenzie (various dates), relating to annual production, operating and capital costs, revenues and prices.

reducing the number of subsequent improvements required; and c) keeping the same management team throughout the project to ensure that the original project philosophy and aims were maintained (Anonymous, 1987). Clyde for its part, has seen massive savings of £1 billion on its original budget, though much is due to expectations of far greater capital cost inflation being allowed for than was eventually the case. In addition, equipment costs were forced down in the mid-1980s as development activity became depressed in the face of plummeting oil prices.

### Conclusions

The findings presented here confirm the message of previous research. North Sea oil projects to develop the largest fields in the northern and central parts of the British sector, possess all the features that characterize inflexibility. Moreover, the adoption of large-scale, complex oil technology, early in the life of North Sea exploration, has resulted in high technical and social costs. Although the rapidity with which British oil resources have been developed cannot be denied, any success on economic grounds would seem to owe much to fortuitously high oil prices. This particularly apples to the 'first generation' of North Sea fields where high oil prices during the mid-1970s and early 1980s have masked the true cost of development. Bearing this in mind, the management of the projects may be considered to be poor, in line with the predictions of past studies. The message to be drawn from this chapter relates to the desirability of small versus large changes in policy. Thus it is suggested that improved decision-making is more likely to be achieved if the processes and outputs of policy possess the virtue of flexibility.

One might ask how relevant all this is to the current and future practice of decision-making both in the North Sea and in other policy arenas and also at both governmental and corporate levels of activity. In the preceding section, some reference was made to ways in which technical decisions in the North Sea's Alwyn North field have been made in such a manner as to make corrective action easier to apply. This change in the general approach to technical developments can be witnessed in other more recently developed fields (e.g. Shell's Kittiwake field) and has been implemented by the field operator. The chapter has also noted the ability of smaller, independent firms to innovate more flexible and modular technical responses to the challenge of the North Sea, even during its earliest pioneering phase. In terms of the literature on business decision-making, this provides support for those such as Quinn (1980) who advocate the implementation of relatively small-scale decisions as a means for pursuing even quite ambitious objectives. Such an approach enhances flexibility, reduces the scale of any errors made and affords decision makers the opportunity to learn inexpensively from their mistakes and experiences. While the implementation of technical decisions in the North Sea has been the direct result of corporate decision-making, it is clear that the role of government is crucially influential. Hence, although one major factor in changing corporate attitudes towards technical choices for development has been lower oil prices, the extent to which government policy can encourage better technical decisions is an issue that must be addressed. In the UK, the early period of North Sea activity saw inappropriate decisions. The kinds of

**Table 2.4 Internal rate of return (%) for selected North Sea oil fields under various scenarios (pre-tax)**

| Field | Historical Oil Prices | 2% pa Real Rises in Prices | £10/bbl ($16) RealPrices |
|---|---|---|---|
| Argyll | 54 | -7 | 6 |
| Auk | 57 | -3 | 5 |
| Beryl A | 44 | 13 | 13 |
| Brent | 24 | 11 | 10 |
| Forties | 58 | 32 | 39 |
| Piper | 72 | 38 | 51 |
| Alwyn N. | -19 | -2 | -44 |
| Buchan | 36 | 5 | -2 |
| Clyde | 15 | 17 | 14 |
| Cormorant | 17 | 12 | 4 |
| Duncan | 35 | -288 | -66 |
| Dunlin | 53 | 17 | 18 |
| Heather | 15 | -22 | -54 |
| Maguus | 38 | 26 | 17 |
| Maureen | 30 | 14 | 4 |
| Montrose | 34 | 0 | - 14 |
| Ninian | 45 | 12 | 10 |
| Statfjord UK | 42 | 25 | 19 |
| Thistle | 38 | 7 | 4 |

*Source*: Calculations are made from data contained in County NatWest Woodmac's North Sea surveys, Wood Mackenzie data and on the basis of the net present value figures presented in Table 2.3 above.

technology selected during the early 1970s thus reflected the untempered rush towards rapid development during this period and were clearly influenced by the nature of government policies designed to achieve this. In particular, the operation of licensing, depletion, taxation and R&D policies served to ensure that almost all the very largest fields were developed first. Moreover, the large multinationals were favoured by the civil servants responsible for making the discretionary licence awards. This, together with the mechanics of the tax system created a very unfortunate situation regarding the role of smaller companies and technical development. Effectively, the very firms most likely to try more experimental technological solutions to development in the cause of greater cost savings were excluded from affairs by the aforementioned bias towards larger companies in licensing and a tax system which actually rewarded wasteful spending. The relative comfort of the major oil companies' position at this time did little to advance the cause of technical learning, at least not towards more flexible means of development.

Recent changes in government policy and expertise, though connected with the maturing of the North Sea and the smaller size of fields to be developed, may be considered to have placed greater emphasis on the need for more flexible and lower-cost technologies. The requirement that licensees support R&D into offshore technology by British firms, the greater diversity which exists mainly because civil servants have become less wary of granting licences to smaller firms (possibly due to the smaller size of fields to be explored) and the generally greater stability of recent government policy have all made a contribution in this respect. Other possible actions could further the development of the kinds of incremental technologies, which the prescriptions discussed in this book favour. These might include the more explicit recognition of the importance of flexibility in technical choice through positive discrimination towards those proposals featuring more incremental technology. Further, the role of independent operators could be made more secure by measures seeking to enhance diverse participation at the industry level, through anti-trust legislation or licensing by auction, for example.

In sum, the findings of this chapter echo those in other areas of technology previously examined and referred to above. High capital intensity, long lead time, large unit size and dependence on specialized infrastructure are all characteristics of inflexible technology projects. Such projects are unlikely to perform successfully in financial terms, except by historical accident. Technical choice should therefore be more incremental, flexible and modular in character. For this to be achieved, careful and continual consideration of the appropriate balance between government intervention and inaction and reliance on market forces is required.

Certain notions from the social construction of technology (SCOT) approach, such as momentum, reverse salients and interpretative flexibility, may be deployed advantageously to further illuminate issues of technology development connected to North Sea oil exploration. The rapid exploitation of UK North Sea oil and gas resources was discussed in terms of a supra-organizational sense of mission, which helped to give impetus and urgency to activities in the early 1970s. Momentum, however, more expressly refers to the idea that there are multiple system components, at least potentially, which need to be brought together collectively for that system to become established. So, the scale of a venture such as is represented by North Sea oil commitments necessitates the input of governmental decision-makers in a particular way. Investments would have looked quite different (presumably) if licensing decisions, for instance, had not favoured such a 'big bang', rapid depletion policy, with larger licensed blocks than was typically the case hitherto and elsewhere. As far as the participation of the major international oil companies was concerned, this is readily understood by reference to their need for new supplies of crude oil, especially in a province where the political and regulatory regime was likely to be friendlier than in increasingly assertive OPEC countries. The benevolence of provisions for capital allowances and the sharing of the 'take' from North Sea oil activities, helped to attract oil company financing. Moreover, the 'bonanza' effect would contribute to the painting of a rosier picture to sell to would-be external financiers (although smaller companies would continue to find such sources of finance difficult to come by).

At this point, a second useful notion may be applied, that of reverse salients. In applying the notion of reverse salients to the case of North Sea oil, the availability of system components such as administrative decision-making, offshore field operators (mainly the major oil companies) and finance have been noted. However, the unevenness of momentum in North Sea activities is clearly indicated by the fledgling state of technical expertise relevant to the exploration, production and transportation of oil from the deepest and most inhospitable oil province to be developed up to that point. The poverty of technical solutions at the beginning of the 1970s, say, contrasts markedly with the development of other system components at that stage of the North Sea venture. The abundance of sheer will and capital served to place severe burdens on scientists and technicians to find the required answers. Yet the momentum of the whole exercise plus the scale of the funds available militated against due consideration of the cost effectiveness of the technical options involved. Rather noticeably, fields operated by independent oil companies displayed a greater tendency to incorporate cost-saving technical solutions to production and transportation. These companies were less able to afford the up-front expenditures that the 'majors' could contemplate and, in Argyll field, for example, bucked the trend of conventional platform development by utilizing a semi-submersible, floating platform. Unfortunately, for the large part, making good the deficiencies in technological capability, in the early years of North Sea field development, tended to mean a rather extreme form of 'throwing money at the problem', encouraged by an over-generous system of capital allowances. The 'problem', as it were, was duly 'solved' and history documents that the oil came ashore in vast quantities, earning vast revenues. However, as was demonstrated above, this achievement was at quite some cost. Certainly approaches favouring more incremental, or cost-effective technical solutions were marginalized. This points up the notion of interpretative flexibility noted above. On one hand, North Sea oil could be portrayed as the saviour of the British economy, a boon which needed to be exploited as rapidly as possible, particularly given OPEC's rising power; even if this necessitated the development of pioneering technology, this in itself was viewed as symbolic of success. On the other hand, the view that tended to be marginalized was that of the greater abundance of oil into the 21st century than was accepted under the dominant consensus, other potentially available and low-cost energy sources such as gas or renewables, and therefore the opportunity to proceed more gradually with North Sea oil. The latter view was more consonant with a policy of ongoing learning about the effectiveness and efficiency of alternative options for production technology but tended not to receive much of a hearing.

Finally, a network perspective suggests that successful inter-firm relations are best characterized by a mutual orientation, trust, endurance and high reciprocity in the exchange of knowledge and production. The early years of North Sea development appear to be lacking in some of these respects, a reflection of the different experiences and practices of US and UK engineers and technicians, for example. This could help to explain some of the problems incurred in project management at this time and also provides a first glance of something less than the harmonious network relations usually portrayed in literature on the topic of inter-firm relations. This issue is to the fore and discussed at greater length in the next case study, of the construction of the Channel Tunnel.

## References

Anonymous (1987), 'First oil for Alwyn North', *Petroleum Times,* December, p. 10.

Balogh, Lord (1974), 'The North Sea Oil Blunder', *The Banker*, vol. 124, pp. 281-288.

Benn, T. (1980), *Arguments for Socialism*, Penguin, Harmondsworth.

Collingridge, D. and James, P. (1989 a), 'Technology, organizations and incrementalism large irrigation schemes in developing countries', *working paper as part of the Diseconomies of Scale In Production Systems Project* carried out jointly by Aston and Warwick Universities and funded by the Leverhulme Foundation.

Collingridge, D. and James, P. (1989 b), 'Technology, organizations and incrementalism: high rise system building in the UK', *Technology Analysis and Strategic Management,* vol. 1, pp. 79-97.

County NatWest Woodmac (various dates), *North Sea Service,* National Westminster Investment Bank Group, Edinburgh.

Craven-Walker, A. (1973), 'How B.P. will equip the North Sea's Forties field', *World Oil,* no. 176, 6 May, pp. 55-58.

Department of Energy (various annual editions), *Development of the Oil and Gas Resources of the United Kingdom*, HMSO, London.

Department of Energy (1976), *North Sea Costs Escalation Study*, Energy Paper no. 7,

HMSO, London.
Department of Energy (1978), Energy Policy: A Consultative Document, HMSO, London.
Department of Energy (1989), *Development of the Oil and Gas Resources of the United Kingdom* HMSO, London.
Department of Energy (1990), *Development of the Oil and Gas Resources of the United Kingdom* HMSO, London.
Fetters, J.K. (1971), 'Here's What Phillips Learned About Drilling in the North Sea', *Oil and Gas Journal,* vol. 69, 9 August, pp. 76-86.
Fier, G.D. (1972), 'The Next Exploration Technique in the North Sea', *Oil and Gas Journal,* vol. 70, 10 April, p. 160.
Hann, D. (1986), 'The Process of Government and UK Oil Participation Policy', *Energy Policy,* vol. 14, pp. 253-261.
Heaney, J. (1973), 'Development of Auk and Brent', *Petroleum Review,* vol. 27, pp. 259-264.
House of Commons Energy Committee (1987), *Session 1986/87, The Effect of Oil and Gas Prices on Activity in the North Sea,* HMSO, London.
Howell, D. (1980), *Hansard,* 23 July.
Kennedy, J.L. (1974), 'North Sea Report', *Oil and Gas Journal,* vol. 72, 3 June, pp. 200-202.
Lynch, J.F. (1965), 'North Sea Poses New Problems in Pipeline Engineering', *Oil and Gas Journal,* vol. 63, 2 August, pp. 113-116.
Lynk, E. (1988), 'The Depletion of UK North Sea Oil', *Scottish Journal of Political Economy,* vol. 35, pp. 313-333.
Mackay, D. I. and Mackay, G.A. (1975), *The Political Economy of North Sea Oil,* Martin Robertson, London.
Noreng, O. (1980), *The Oil Industry and Government Strategy in the North Sea,* Croom Helm, London.
Odell, P. (1986) *Oil And World Power* (8th edition), Penguin, London.
Odell, P. and Rosing, K. (1977), 'Optimal Development of the North Sea's Oil Fields - the Reply (to the Critique of Wall *et al.)*', *Energy Policy,* vol. 5, p. 305.
Odell, P. and Rosing, K. (1980), *The Future of Oil,* Kogan Page, London.
Quinn, J.B. (1980), *Strategies for Change: Logical Incrementalism,* Irwin, Homewood, Ill.
Reid, R.G. (1987), 'A View of European Oil and Gas Issues', in J. Rees and P. Odell (eds.), *The International Oil Industry,* Macmillan, London, pp. 76-87.
Robinson, C. (1981), 'The Errors of North Sea Policy', *Lloyds Bank Review,* no. 141, pp. 14-33.
Robinson, C. (1982), 'Oil Depletion Policy in the United Kingdom', *Three Banks Review,* no. 135, pp. 8-15.
Robinson, C. (1990), 'Successes and Failures in British Government North Sea Policy', paper presented at *25 Years of the North Sea,* Conference at Surrey University, 23 March.
Robinson, C. and Morgan, J. (1978), *North Sea Oil in the Future,* Macmillan, London.
Sampson, A. (1988), The Seven Sisters (2nd edition), Coronet, London.
Scott, R.W. (1972), 'The North Sea: Offshore's Greatest Venture', *World Oil,* 15 August, pp. 33-40 and pp. 136-139.
Trimble, N. (1976), 'The Costs of North Sea Oil Developments: Past Trends and Future Prospects', *North Sea Occasional Paper No. 10,* University of Aberdeen Department of Political Economy, Aberdeen.
UKOOA (United Kingdom Offshore Operators' Association) (1999), *Oil and Gas:*

*Economic Contribution - 1999 Economic Report*, www.ukooa.co.uk.
Wildavsky, A. and Tannenbaum, E. (1981), *The Politics of Mistrust*, Sage, London.

# 3 Channel Tunnel

## Introduction

The idea of a fixed link between Britain and France was mooted early in the seventeenth century when the Amiens Academy in France launched a competition to find better ways of crossing the English Channel (Bedelian, 1995). A proposal for a tunnel under the English Channel came in 1802 when the idea was put before Napoleon and at least 26 other proposals were rejected from that time up to the late 1970s, principally because of concerns over national security. In 1973 work had begun on a pilot phase of a government-guaranteed project. However, failure to ratify the Treaty resulted in the project being cancelled in 1975, due to a lack of public funding and escalating costs (Fisher, 1993). Vickerman (1994) notes that the lack of an independent 'champion', able to exercise both political and financial influence, was a major factor in the project's collapse. Although the scheme was officially abandoned in 1975, pressure from three main sources still existed. First the private sector was hungry for major new projects for both construction and financial organizations. Second, the European Commission was keen to improve European transport networks. (Indeed, these two worked together on a report for the Commission by Coopers and Lybrand on the subject.) Thirdly, the two national railway companies put forward their own scheme for a single small bore tunnel in 1978. Hence the idea for a tunnel was resurrected and by 1984 a group of contractors and banks had set up the Channel Tunnel Group. This development was coupled with the setting up of an equivalent French group (Francemanche SA) and together, as CTG-FM, they submitted a proposal for a twin bored rail tunnel scheme, based upon an earlier proposal from the 1970s. (This was in October, 1985 and followed an 'Invitation to Promoters' issued by the British and French Governments in February, 1985.) The British response to the CTG-FM proposal was to concern itself with the feasibility of private finance, while the French started to conduct regional level consultations to prepare for a rapid conclusion of the public inquiries necessary under the French planning system. A group of banks examined the financial feasibility of the proposal and concluded in favour of the CTG-Francemanche rail tunnel scheme, but reported that guarantees were imperative for successful financing (Vickerman, 1994). Margaret Thatcher and Francois Mitterand gave their support to the Channel Tunnel scheme in January 1986 and in February of that year the Treaty of Canterbury was signed, which gave intergovernmental sanction for a fixed link. This treaty was later ratified by the UK and France in July 1987, and a concession was formally awarded to CTG-FM on 14 March 1986. Contrary to the wishes of the promoters of the project there were to be no governmental financial guarantees for the project, the financing of which was to be left to the market. The building contractors which had been so much a part of CTG-Francemanche separated from this consortium and formed the Anglo-French joint venture TransManche Link (TML), which in May 1986 was awarded the contract to design, build and commission the tunnel, for clients (Eurotunnel, Britain and Eurotunnel, France) that at the time were no more than two pieces of paper. CTG-FM later became the British and French subsidiaries of Eurotunnel, which was incorporated in September 1986. Eurotunnel did not acquire 'a mind of its own' until October 1986 when the delayed Equity 2 share issue was made. The share issue was conditional upon the promoters of the project, the banks and the building contractors, giving up control of Eurotunnel, so permitting the entry of institutional investors and an independent majority on its board (Benard and Morton, 1989). This was almost nine months after the award of the Concession to CTG-FM and five months after TML was awarded the Construction Contract. The Equity 3 flotation brought together various agreements, legislation and contracts plus the marketing and equity package for the project and took place on what became known as 'Impact Day'. Hence the twinned companies were floated on the London and Paris stock exchanges in 16 November, 1987, just a month after the 'Black Monday' global stock market crash, which could have undone the whole thing (Benard and Morton, 1989). Eurotunnel supplanted CTG-FM as the holder of the 55-year design, construct and operating concession (since extended to 99 years), and was faced with a construction contract drawn up before their birth. (At the end of the concession the project will revert to the two governments.) The absence of an operator in place as a client from the outset of the project has been referred to as a 'polo mint' project structure (Morton, 1995a). This, and its implications for design, development and the overall management of the project is a key issue for discussion below.

The chapter is organized as follows. The next section presents an analysis of the inflexibility of the Channel Tunnel project. As with the North Sea oil case study discussed in the previous chapter four indicators (capital intensity, lead time, unit size and dependence upon specialized infrastructure) are applied to analyze the extent to which the project may be deemed inflexible. Following this, the third section first assesses aspects of the policy-making process relating to the capacity of various groups to voice dissent over the setting up of the concession, the Construction Contract and technical design. It then goes on to examine aspects of conflict and mutual adjustment between Eurotunnel and TransManche Link. The penultimate section draws together various financial issues and assesses the performance of the project based on the development of a number of alternative scenarios and the conduct of discounted cash flow analysis. The concluding section summarizes the main themes and findings from the study.

## Analyzing Inflexibility

The Channel Tunnel is the result of very high capital expenditure, and several years of construction, before any revenues from the service could be recovered. Eurotunnel was established as an independent company to finance the project. The majority of the financing is based on a large syndicated banking loan with equity accounting for approximately 20% of the project finance. The costs of the project have been estimated to be approximately £10 billion (Morton, 1995b) - about double the original 1986 proposed estimate. The rising costs have been financed by additional loans and several rights issues. Table 3.1 shows estimated capital costs for the project and illustrates its highly capital intensive nature. The Channel Tunnel project's high capital intensity parallels the findings from the study of the development of early U.K. North Sea oil fields discussed in Chapter 2, above. For the Channel Tunnel the original 1987 estimate was for capital intensity was 75%, and a further rise to 82% (due to the increasing construction costs) reinforces the point, the cash flow implications of which are considered below.

In terms of unit size, the Channel Tunnel constituted at its inception the largest privatized project in the world. Although at 50km the tunnel is not the world's longest railway tunnel, its 38km under sea was a record at the time of construction. Building large units slows learning about new technology, as there is less operating data that can be drawn on. Indeed, with the Channel Tunnel, the uniqueness of the geology, with tunnelling in chalk, left a limited capacity for transferring knowledge from other tunnelling projects (Robbins, 1995). The lead time from start of construction to the start of operations was planned to be five-and-a-half years - from December 1987 to May 1993. Table 3.2 highlights the major milestones in terms of the time taken from the granting of the concession to the date when the tunnel was operational. The figure given for the beginning of construction does not include work on infrastructure that took place before December 1987. For example, work began in late 1986 on the Isle of Grain factory that supplied concrete lining segments. The overall lead time achieved from the ratification of the Treaty granting the Concession to the granting of the final operating certificate is given in columns B-D in Table 3.2, and was 89 months. The remainder of this section provides an investigation of the dedicated infrastructure required for the Channel Tunnel project.

**Table 3.1 Capital intensity of the Channel Tunnel (estimates of 1987 and 1994 compared)**

| | Capital cost (£ million) | Operating cost (£ million) | Total cost (£ million) | Capital intensity |
|---|---|---|---|---|
| 1987 | 5,250 | 1,769 | 7,019 | 75% |
| 1994 | 10,116 | 2,185 | 12,301 | 82% |

*Sources:* 1987 estimates based on data cited in the Eurotunnel Prospectus (1987: 54). 1994 estimates based on data cited in the Eurotunnel Rights Issue, 1994 document, page 48. Costs have been discounted at 15% per annum.

The construction of the Channel Tunnel has necessitated the use of specialized state-of-the-art equipment for preparing drilling samples (in order to determine the site's geology), or to make the railway system operational, for example. This technology could be deemed state-of-the-art, but it should be noted that, initially, it was primarily based on that used in earlier attempts and other tunnels. However, each tunnel project requires different and specialized technology to suit the unique geology through which the tunnel is bored. As referred to above the first step in the actual construction of the UK end of the tunnel involved the building of a factory on a site close to the Folkestone terminal to make the segments used to line the tunnel. The segments weighed nine tons each and required high quality concrete (Fisher, 1993). Indeed, Colin Kirkland, Technical Director of Eurotunnel between 1985 and 1991, stated that the concrete lining segments would be at the high technology end of the project as a variety of lining types were available. For example, where ground pressures are higher, tunnels require thicker lining segments. However, as the internal diameter of the tunnel had to remain the same, a larger void was required to be excavated, necessitating the use of larger boring machines (Jones, 1987).

**Table 3.2 Lead times for Channel Tunnel development**

| A<br>Project officially sanctioned [a] | B<br>Concession granted [b] | C<br>Construction begins [c] | D<br>Operations begin [d] | B-D | C-D |
|---|---|---|---|---|---|
| | | | | (time in months) | |
| Jan 1986 | Jul 1987 | Dec 1987 | Dec 1994 | 89 | 84 |

*Notes*: a. Date of governmental sanction for the project is given in Jones (1987: 65).
b. The concession granted date is taken from Eurotunnel Prospectus and refers to the month in which the Treaty of Canterbury was ratified (1987: 7).
c. The date for the start of construction applies to the first driving of the seaward tunnel the UK side.
d. The operations commencement date is taken from the Chairman's letter in the Eurotunnel annual report 1994 (Eurotunnel, 1995a, page 5), where it states that 'the management team..took Eurotunnel...to the fourth and final operating certificate, issued to us on 15 December 1994'. Although limited services were offered before this date, it is felt that the system became fully operational once all four services were commissioned.

The three tunnels were excavated by 11 full-face tunnel boring machines, five French and six British. Each machine cost approximately £7 million in 1989 prices (The Independent, 1989). The TBMs were constructed in at least eight different diameters, depending on whether they were to work under land or sea, how the tunnel was lined and the anticipated geology. Among tunnellers the machine design is considered one of the more interesting parts of the project, being literally at the forefront or cutting edge of technology. The machines ordered were supplied by people who essentially designed the machines used in the abortive 1970s scheme. It is generally accepted that the TBMs used on the project were based on a previous design but incorporated increased sophistication such as telescoping bodies as the excavation proceeds. For example, a Robbins machine delivered in 1974 and never used, although well maintained, could not be used in the 1987 scheme due to technological advances in the intervening years (Jones, 1987). On the UK side the TBMs required modification after boring had started due to wet ground that held up the tunnel drives. Previous geological surveys had not highlighted the fissured chalk that allowed water to pour into the workings. The modifications required meant that the tunnels, already several weeks behind schedule, had to be shut down for a further three weeks to make costly modifications. In the words of Richard Robbins (Vice Chairman of Robbins - the company that built the boring machines) chances were taken 'with cutting-edge technology beyond the demonstrated state-of-the-art at the time' (Robbins, 1995). The implications of this were the time and expense needed to see through the de-bugging process. Due to fears that the middle and lower chalk beds on the French side could not be grouted effectively (grouting was required to cope with the wet ground encountered), a completely different approach and increasingly sophisticated and complicated machinery were employed in comparison to work on the British side. (A closed pressure bulkhead shield was used to advance the boring.) However, as it turned out, the chalk formations in question could have been grouted effectively with existing open-type, unpressurized shields. Thus equipment that dated from 1974 could have succeeded, would have reduced the cost and time of tunnelling start-up and avoided the complexity of the machines that were used. The problem was that from the information that was to hand there was a danger that grouting might not be effective and that the work would fall behind the tight schedule for tunnelling. Thus Robbins (1995) states that the complexity of the tunnel boring machines stemmed from the requirement for high rates of advance. The price paid for the prototype nature of the machines was, ironically, a late start to tunnelling and a long period of debugging.

Behind the tunnel boring machines a further 200 metres of vital back-up equipment extended down the tunnel with conveyors near the ceiling and supply wagons on rails on the floor. Close to the machine were segment erection systems with which a small crane placed and then wedged segments into position by means of a tapered keystone. This allowed the strength of the rock to contribute to the strength of the linings and provided a smooth finish requiring little further treatment. Electronic distance measuring and lasers were required for the surveying underground, as the consequences of going off-line were too complicated to contemplate. Only one company had the advanced system that complied with the detailed specification (it won a Queen's award for technological achievement in 1986). This high technology had to be robust to combine such qualities with delicate electronics sensitive to ever-present moisture, dust and temperature variations. The aforementioned operations were characterized by high automation, with sophisticated computerized systems coordinating crane and train movements as well as monitoring operations.

Once the tunnelling was completed, a massive operation to install the fixed equipment took place. Power supplies, tracks, communications and mechanical systems were installed for the transportation network. Here, the Intergovernmental Commission (IGC) imposed major safety-related changes to the designs submitted in the 1987 Concession agreement. (The Treaty of Canterbury set up the IGC to coordinate the British and French governments' approach to the project and to handle questions relating to the construction, operation and safety of the tunnel). This resulted in a rise of 94% in the proposed costs (see 'Fixed Equipment' in Table 3.3). The tunnel also required three undersea pumping stations, which collect water from sumps and pump it to treatment plants on each coast. In addition, other permanent installations included specialized ventilation and cooling systems.

The Eurotunnel fleet required specialized shuttles considerably more sophisticated than those used on similar links - e.g. the Swiss Vereina Tunnel (Jones, 1987). The double-deck shuttles were the largest passenger-carrying trains built to date and the electric locomotives at each end of the shuttle train are among the most powerful locomotives used in Europe. These trains were developed specifically for the Channel Tunnel project over a four-year period. The fleet is coordinated via a single control centre at Folkestone and the extremely demanding performance required meant that the latest electronic technology had to be employed for the control centre. The rolling stock also experienced severe cost increases due to design changes imposed by the IGC. For example, at one stage, final approvals for a safety related option of widening of pedestrian doors in a passenger train car from 600 mm to 700 mm were not forthcoming from the IGC. At this point the changes would have cost £5.8 million and TML continued with the manufacturing phase to keep on schedule. However, the IGC later decided that the 600 mm doors were unacceptable which resulted in a £45 million cost increase and a nine-month delay to change. Perhaps the most vital infrastructure in terms of the financial viability of the project is that of the rail links to Folkestone and Sangatte. Eurotunnel requires a high-speed rail link from London to Paris if it is to effectively compete against equivalent air transportation - a factor calculated into the financial assessment of the Channel Tunnel. The French have built a high- speed link to Lille, while a similar link on the British side is not expected to be completed until 2007 at the earliest (DETR, 2000).

To summarize, the Channel Tunnel project clearly possesses the four indicators of inflexibility cited above. The project is highly capital intensive. Long lead time is indicated by the several years taken from the granting of the Concession to all four services being granted final operating certificates. In terms of unit size, a record was set for the longest undersea tunnel built, and the project has demanded the use of specialized, dedicated

**Table 3.3 Channel Tunnel project costs (running totals and % change)**

| | 1987 | 1990 | 1994 | 1998 | Increase 1987-98 |
|---|---|---|---|---|---|
| Construction: | | | | | |
| Tunnels | 1814 | 2836 | 3212 | 3212 | 77 |
| Terminals | 661 | 763 | 842 | 842 | 27 |
| Fixed Equipment | 939 | 1223 | 1826 | 1826 | 94 |
| Rolling Stock | 334 | 823 | 1073 | 1073 | 221 |
| Bonuses/ Contingency | 515 | 98 | 70 | 70 | -86 |
| Direct works | - | - | 55 | 55 | n/a |
| Total costs of construction | 4263 | 5743 | 7078 | 7078 | 66 |
| Finance-related Costs: | | | | | |
| Owner's costs | 852 | 700 | 1090 | 1128 | 32 |
| Adjustments for inflation | 621 | 1178 | 1047 | 1146 | 85 |
| Finance fees/costs | 1293 | 1584 | 2009 | 4979 | 285 |
| Net cash flow | - | 224 | - | - 1859 | n/a |
| Transfer to interest reserves | - | - | - | 72 | n/a |
| Total financing costs | 2766 | 3686 | 4146 | 5466 | 97 |
| Total Costs | 7029 | 9429 | 11224 | 12544 | 78 |

*Sources*: 1987 calculations based on data from Eurotunnel Rights Issue document 1990 (p. 28 for construction costs, p. 22 for financing costs). 1990 calculations based on construction cost data taken from Eurotunnel Rights Issue document 1994 (p. 33) and financing cost data from Eurotunnel Rights Issues document 1990 (p. 34). 1994 and 1998 calculations based on data from Eurotunnel Rights Issue document 1994 (p. 33 for construction costs, p. 34 for financing costs). N.B. All figures converted to 1994 prices, data indexed from Retail Price Index (Annual Abstract of Statistics 1995, p. 336).

infrastructure. These indicators provide a type of shorthand for reading the momentum and reverse salients associated with developing a major infrastructure project. One may ask what organizational and public policy factors are implicated with such a development, or served to exacerbate the problems of construction and financing associated with it. These issues are addressed in the following section.

## The Policy-making Process and Contractual Issues

This section addresses aspects of the policy-making process and contractual issues associated with the development of the fixed link scheme. First, the UK government's involvement is assessed, particularly with regard to the award of the Concession, the extent of debate concerning the implications of the operation of the link and its influence (through the Bank of England) on the willingness of financial institutions to support the chosen scheme. Subsequently, the focus of the section switches to examine the relationship between Eurotunnel, the 'client' in the Channel Tunnel project and TML, the group of firms which together comprised the 'contractor' responsible for design, construction, testing and commissioning of the tunnel. Here, there are two principal concerns relating to proposition (ii) stated previously. One is to assess the extent to which the Channel Tunnel project represents a case where the development of inflexible technology projects has been associated with centralized decision-making processes. This facet of the discussion turns upon a consideration of Eurotunnel, nominally the promoter of the scheme in question, as a 'missing actor', a key stakeholder absent from the negotiation table when critical decisions likely to have a bearing on the management of the project and its economics were being made. The second concern addresses the connection between the contractual arrangements governing the development of the Channel Tunnel, the differing objectives of the client and the contractor, and the implications of this for the promotion of mutual collaboration (or 'partnering'). Of interest are the different interpretations views of design held by the parties (c.f. the notion of interpretative flexibility). A third area of interest is the extent to which the project relies on public sector finance, which would undermine claims about its status as a private sector venture.

The genesis of the Channel Tunnel project can be described as anything but smooth. As early as 1980, the principle was established that the project should be privately financed and that the British government would give a viable scheme a 'fair go'. At this stage, intending promoters raised their profiles by putting forth their individual schemes. A formal 'Invitation to Promoters' was issued by the British and French Governments on 2 April 1985. The then Transport Secretary, Mr. Nicholas Ridley assured MPs that guidelines would 'ensure that there is adequate public consultation, that environmental, social and employment impacts are fully appreciated and that the financial conditions are fully met', with the two governments considering all of these issues before reaching their decisions (Jones, 1987). Essentially, the invitation: a) gave details of the guarantee against cancellation for political reasons while repeating that no other would be given; b) promised that the British Government would use its 'best endeavours' to get the necessary legislation through; c) outlined road and rail improvements which would be necessary on either side of the Channel; d) committed both nations to the speediest possible customs and immigration checks; e) required promoters to supply financial 'evidence of robustness and viability', explaining how and when large a sum would be raised; and f) set out details of what was to be built, the construction timetable and a breakdown of costs.

Once the 'Invitation to Promoters' was published coalitions of interests manoeuvred in an attempt to forward their interests and gain the upper hand. Debate concerning the need for a tunnel had been widespread - unions officials were concerned about job losses on the ferries, environmentalists about the damage to the Kent countryside, ferry operators disliked the added competition, and various people were generally opposed to the thought of a fixed link. However, as Jones (1987) notes, up to the time that a particular scheme was chosen, the protests against a fixed link were fragmented, and at no time did a single opposition movement take shape, with each community preferring to present its own case. The extent to which the House of Commons could formulate an independent viewpoint was also questioned. A furore in the Commons developed over a television report highlighting the claim that a sizeable number of MPs were being paid as 'consultants' by the promoters of rival schemes or by opponents to a fixed link. Although those declaring an interest were only a small percentage, this factor helps to highlight areas where MPs may have been handicapped in formulating independent viewpoints while being funded by large business organizations whose interests would be advanced by sympathetic MPs. The Speaker told the House that 'every MP knows if he has an enterprise it should be registered. It is a matter of honour' (Jones, 1987). That weekend the Observer newspaper reported that 37 peers and MPs had business ties with the consortia or opponents - although this did not mean they personally supported a particular scheme or had a direct financial interest. As mentioned above CTG-FM won the concession for the fixed link in March 1986. One characterization of the process leading up to this event suggests an appeal to rational, technical and economic criteria. On this view, the two governments favoured the tunnel scheme due to the relative simplicity of their financial arrangements. Cost overruns and time delays were perceived as being less harmful than on alternative schemes. In addition, the tunnel scheme included the UK and French national railways, providing the scheme with extra financial strength as rail passengers would automatically be directed through the Tunnel. Furthermore, the House of Commons Select Committee rejected alternatives (namely the Eurobridge, Euroroute and the Channel Expressway) as they did not think their proposed technologies were proven. Another perspective builds an account of the political behaviour of large organizations seeking to exploit links with the British Government in order to secure the concession. According to the Channel Tunnel Group's Nicholas Henderson, the final days before a winner was announced saw rounds of bargaining at an ever-quickening pace. The winner was decided as a result of last minute trade-offs between politicians and business people. Technical specifications, traffic forecasts and cost projections seemed irrelevant and Nicholas Ridley played the role of conductor, suggesting combinations and alterations to schemes that would improve their chances (Jones, 1987).

Once the CTG-FM scheme was chosen there was a need to secure the approval of Parliament for the project and to attend to the formality of concluding a Concession Agreement. In addition, for the CTG-FM scheme to proceed an equally vital element depended upon a newly incorporated Eurotunnel raising the finance for the construction of the tunnel. A large syndicated loan package put together the majority of the financing (80%) for a proposed six-year construction period and totalled £5 billion (Vickerman, 1989). (The European Investment Bank additionally provided one billion pounds in credit.) However, the loan agreement depended upon raising approximately 20% of the project's cost in equity. Equity I was taken up by promoting banks and construction companies. Equity II was a private placing of more than £206 million in late 1986, at a time when the Channel Tunnel Bill was in its Committee stage. Despite a substantial shortfall in the take up, and a hostile reception by some financial analysts, the Equity II issue was underwritten. Equity III was a public flotation in November 1987, a month after the stock market crash, which raised over £770 million. And a further rights issue in November 1990 raised another

£560 million, although this could only go ahead after the banking syndicate had, somewhat reluctantly, agreed to lend Eurotunnel a further £2 billion.

Once the scheme was chosen, the Department of Transport and Eurotunnel supported a Bill approving details of the scheme and ratifying the Treaty with France which would be put through both Houses of Parliament in turn, with Royal Assent being necessary before the consortium could issue shares. The Bill would be a 'hybrid', a special type of measure used when a matter of public policy directly affects private interests. Usually in Britain, major public projects are subject to a public inquiry into the scheme's financial viability, environmental impact and safety levels. The hybrid Bill allowed both the private and the public aspects of construction to be dealt with in a single piece of parliamentary legislation. This procedure has been claimed to have the effect of removing substantial rights from the individual to make representations against a privately-financed scheme compared with the case where the scheme is financed by the public sector. Alternatively, Vickerman (1989) has suggested that the

> Select Committee procedure involves a more searching examination than do Public Inquiries, especially of government intentions, and since the detail of the scheme is incorporated as part of an Act of Parliament, it becomes less easy for the developer to make changes.

Eurotunnel claimed that the timetable imposed by the British Government from inception to Royal Assent of the Bill was 'grotesquely tight for a scheme of this magnitude' (Jones, 1987).

Throughout the Select Committee's examination of the scheme the ferry operators contrived to set much of the agenda. Indeed, counsel for the Government attempted to have them ruled out of order, condemning their case as an 'assault on the principles of the Bill' (Jones, 1987). The most notable but ultimately apparent success of the ferry operators' opposition was their influence in getting written into the Bill an undertaking that no government subsidy could be paid to the tunnel operators. In addition, Holliday (1989) notes the willingness of CTG-FM and later Eurotunnel to consult with local groups in Kent about matters such as spoil disposal and employment. Nevertheless, although there was considerable scope for diverse interests to air their views, in consultation with the promoter/client, in parliamentary terms the tight timetable for the Bill, a period of eighteen months, appears to have reduced the extent of debate concerning design and the organizational framework for the project. Moreover, after the Bill's second reading in Parliament, no objections to the basic principle of the project could be raised in committee and only parties with a specific, direct interest could challenge the Bill (Vickerman, 1991). The question remains, however, as to the role of the British government in the financing and support of an ostensibly privately funded project.

In October 1986, Eurotunnel was experiencing difficulties over raising £206 million for its 'Equity II' financing. The attention of Ministers was now focused on the struggle facing Eurotunnel and it seemed that the project faced imminent disaster. The market perceived the issue as having too high a risk, and too low a return in a market too full with other new issues. Indeed, a poll by the Financial Times newspaper between the 23rd and 28th of July 1986 indicated the problems in raising the finance. Using a sample of 25 institutions, less than a quarter indicated that they were going to seriously consider investing in the project. Ten of the 25 fund managers stated that they would not be investing in the scheme and a further nine were undecided (Jones, 1987). The £206 million would not have been forthcoming if the Bank of England and Ministers had not set out on a programme to entice and persuade institutions into coming up with the finance. Jones ponders on 'how much of the intervention could be described as legitimate lobbying by the Bank of England and how much was straight bullying by the UK Government', concluding that 'it is difficult to say, but direct and highly effective intervention there certainly was' (Jones, 1987). In his view the Government was 'arm-twisting' financial institutions with the help of the Bank of England into taking action that the markets may not otherwise have taken.

Commentators such as Marcou (1993) and Vickerman (1991) refer to political guarantees and other forms of support for the Channel Tunnel project that have stopped short of direct commercial or financial guarantees. For example, as mentioned above, the political risks of the rejection of the Treaty of Canterbury by the U.K. parliament due to public opposition to the fixed link were addressed by the British and French Governments, which promised to do their best to facilitate the execution of the Concession Agreement. Also, in August 1990, when the Bank of England was attempting to persuade Japanese financial institutions to increase their involvement in loans for the project, a 'significant' expression of continued support for the project by the U.K. Government was relayed by Prime Minister Mrs. Thatcher to her Japanese counterpart (Marcou, 1993). Further illustrations include the French Government's decision to go ahead with the TGV high-speed rail link connecting the French terminal of the Channel Tunnel to Paris (Vickerman, 1991) and financial support from what was the European Community, through the European Investment Bank, in the form of loans to Eurotunnel.

The politics of the Concession Agreement had implications for project management. Marcou (1993) has analyzed the underlying politics of the Concession Agreement and its related contracts and suggested serious shortcomings in the relationships between the major parties involved. He argues that a prima facie examination of the contractual arrangements could, arguably, identify Eurotunnel to be the promoter of the project. However, the concession was created by TML and the financial institutions mentioned above. These bodies were the *de facto* promoters of the project, particularly since Eurotunnel was only a fledgling organization at the time that the basic contracts were signed (1986). In addition, the majority of Eurotunnel's directors and executives were drawn from companies in the building consortium. This posed no problem by itself. Of greater significance was the extent to which neither the building contractors nor the banks were interested in the operation of the fixed link *per se*. The building contractors' priority was to derive a profit from the Construction Contract and to shed as much risk as possible. They were responsible for the initial proposal, the initial capital for securing the concession, and raising the finance under Equity I to enable the conduct of early design work. However, the provisions of the concession and loan agreements gave the contractors no direct interest in the profitability of the operation of the Channel Tunnel subsequent to handover. Further, reductions in their share of the equity in Eurotunnel fell following the rights issues (from 70% of Eurotunnel's capital in mid-1986 to a 7% stake in 1987, after Equity III) (Vickerman, 1991). The recalcitrance of financial institutions to finance the project has already been mentioned. The extent to which they have become more directly involved in the control of the project relates to the exacerbation, through the spiralling costs of development, of already pronounced banking risks, linked to the high gearing of the project. The differing orientations of the building contractors and the banks have been key to their relations with Eurotunnel at various times during the project, relations that have been shaped by the contractual links between the parties and, indeed, by the process by which contracting was conducted.

For example, the Concession Agreement placed Eurotunnel in contractual links with: a) the British and French governments through the award of the Concession; b) the contractors (TML) through a Construction Contract; c) banking consortium of some 200 banks worldwide, in the form of a loan agreement; and d) the British and French railway companies, BR and SNCF, through a rail usage agreement. These contracts are characterized by an interdependence that placed an emphasis on rapid development. For example, the Concession could only have become operational if the tunnel was financed and built. The Construction Contract depended on the finance being available. The finance depended on the guaranteed revenue from the railways, which in turn depended on the tunnel being ready at a specified time. Again this depended on a minimum of delay during the necessary legislative processes (Vickerman, 1994).

Eurotunnel's contract with TML had three cost categories: target cost for the tunnelling; lump sum for the terminals and the mechanical and electrical works for the tunnel; and the procurement contract for the rolling stock and associated major equipment. It is interesting to consider the view of a member of Eurotunnel's legal team involved in the management of the Construction Contract that the target cost element of the contract was chosen on the basis that

> the ground conditions had been relatively well mapped...people had a relatively good idea as to the type of ground that would be encountered and that, therefore, it was fairly safe to set some form of target which TML were comfortable with and at the same time provide them with the incentive of a bonus for underrunning...costs...I think that the expectation of that time was that there would be an underrunning [of] cost (interview, 1996).

In this area disagreement between Eurotunnel and TML focused on rising tunnelling costs stemming in part from the ground being wetter than expected. In the original 1987 contract, Eurotunnel was responsible for roughly 70% of cost overruns on the original contract, TML was responsible for the remaining 30%, with contribution of the latter being capped at a maximum 6% of the total cost. Thus, in October 1989, Eurotunnel was responsible for approximately £1.3 billion of the tunnelling costs. A revised agreement in 1990 aimed at a fairer distribution of the risks left Eurotunnel responsible for the first £1.58 billion of the costs, and TML responsible for 30% of all above that figure. In addition, TML agreed to reduce procurement costs after they had risen sharply. Eurotunnel paid for the cost of the rolling stock plus a handling fee to TML.

A member of the Disputes Panel for the Channel Tunnel project has reflected upon the difficulties involved in managing the target works. In his view, the problem is one of ensuring that the form of contract employed on a complex project should flow from the nature and uncertainties of the engineering work to be encountered. Hence

> the form of the contract(s) should be built around the engineering , not vice versa. Do not accept blandishments about target contracts eliminating confrontation; they do not where the unforeseen - but not necessarily the unforeseeable - intervenes on a major tunnelling project. Far better to identify the major potential...risks, how to eliminate or at least control them, and to apportion responsibility for the residual risks. Such reasoning then provides the principles for the contractual relationships (interview, 1996).

Interestingly, with this and the initial absence of a client in mind, the belief within Eurotunnel was that the potential for wetter than expected ground conditions should have been recognized from the geological data that TML had in advance of tunnelling work commencing. Also, the design of the boring machines used could have been undertaken on the basis of such an interpretation of the data (financial adviser to Eurotunnel, interview, 1996).

Turning to the lump sum works contract, this referred to the construction of the terminals and the installation of all fixed mechanical and electrical equipment in the terminals, the specification of which could be altered through variation orders. Here, the risks incurred in development were to be borne by the contractors, save for an allowance for inflation in the construction sector, and the lump sum proved to be the source of great conflict over claims by the contractor for recompense for additional costs (Neerhout, 1994). Again, it has been claimed that one of the factors contributing to the choice of the lump sum arrangement was that the technology would be sufficiently well defined so as to enable a fixed price to be set in advance of work, a position that has been seen as 'frankly naive' in retrospect (Anderson and Roskrow, 1994). Another key factor seems to have been the insistence by the banks that the 'least defined portions [of the work], the terminals, and the mechanical and electrical (M&E) equipment ...be done on a lump-sum turnkey basis' (Ratzer, 1995). According to one a member of the Eurotunnel legal team the banks were looking for a level of certainty concerning possible exposure to debt and it was felt that fixing a price for the M&E work was safe, particularly when the banks were already comfortable with the expectation of an underrun on the tunnelling side of things (interview, 1996).

In October, 1989 TML claimed an extra £380 million from Eurotunnel for the cost of changing the design and specification of the fixed equipment work ordered by the client, partly at the behest of the IGC. The Maitre d'Oeuvre oversight group surprised TML by backing Eurotunnel's estimate of £1.48 billion, which although not a binding ruling was seen by TML as an independent assessment of cost which constituted a rock-bottom forecast, rather than a definitive statement of out-turn costs. This outstanding amount was brought to arbitration for settlement, and a partial deal was apparently agreed which persuaded the banks to release sufficient funds to keep the project going for another four months, by which time TML and Eurotunnel were to have reached a proper settlement. The deal in question failed to tackle the key issues connected to the lump sum works, which were left for subsequent arbitration, but included changes to the target and procurement contracts already mentioned above. However, within weeks the project was again facing disaster as TML refused to sign. They wanted Morton out as it was considered that he was a key factor in the deteriorating relationship between the senior management of both companies but believed that moving him from co-chairman to deputy chairman and chief executive involved him even more directly in the construction process. TML then proceeded to take the near bankrupt Eurotunnel to court in France, for non-payment of its monthly account. Only intervention by the Bank of England, resulting in the appointment of John Neerhout as project Chief Executive at Eurotunnel, helped to avert disaster and break the deadlock, though the lump sum disagreement lingered on (Anderson and Roskrow, 1994). Morton remained a co-chairman of the Group.

As far as the procurement contract for the rolling stock is concerned, a key issue was TML's reluctance to get involved in this kind of work, since it was in this aspect of the work that they had least expertise. At the same time that TML might have preferred to have Eurotunnel separately contracting out for the provision of the rolling stock, the view of the banks was that there should be one party, TML, who would take overall responsibility for delivering on the entire project. Bearing this in mind, the procurement contract may be seen as a compromise which enabled the contractor to avoid cost risks on the procurement of the rolling stock, since they would get a fee for the work, while attending to the banks' need for someone to 'point the finger at' (Eurotunnel legal team member, interview 1996). To make matters worse, in addition to TML's lack of expertise regarding rolling stock, the state of the market for rolling stock at the time that the contract was made was such that there little competition for the rolling stock work which led to much higher costs on this activity than were expected (financial adviser to Eurotunnel, interview, 1996).

The problems faced by the project thus partly arose from the process of setting up (and to renegotiate) the Construction Contract and indeed the fact that a single document housed the various methods of compensating the different parts of the work described above. It has been argued that more cost-efficient and better quality project management would have followed from having separate contracts for different aspects of the work with different contractors or groups of contractors, rather than having a single design and build contract with one contractor as occurred (Ratzer, 1995). As indicated above, the influence of the banking consortium on contracting seemed to operate in the direction of a sole document in which the locus of responsibility for delivery of a complete system clearly rested with TML. Another slant on this concerns the degree to which TML retained control over the project as a whole, unease about rolling stock procurement notwithstanding. On this view, having one overall contract made it more difficult for the client, Eurotunnel, to take work away from TML, than under arrangements where there were separate contracts with various contractors (Eurotunnel legal team member, interview, 1996).

The effectiveness of incentives or penalties under the various contract mechanisms to motivate the efficiency of the contractor has been considered to be rather poor. For example the lump sum has been seen as the subject of a TML strategy, from mid-1989 onwards, to get recompense for the M&E work to be converted to a cost-plus basis to cater for cost increases incurred as a result of changes in design specification. This was something that neither the banks nor the Maitre d'Oeuvre were willing to allow though the size of the lump sum was increased. The procurement contract allowed for a fixed fee of 11.5% to be paid to TML for procuring rolling stock and as such offered little incentive to reduce costs. Finally, the target cost contract has been considered to be the 'least disastrous' of the contract mechanisms in operation, while the potential relief of liability that TML would receive upon timely commissioning of the rolling stock did seem to concentrate the mind of the contractor towards the 'hand-over' date. Further, problems with auditing or monitoring made to difficult to specify the level of contractor performance. From Eurotunnel's point of view the size of their auditing team was too small to do the work effectively (and there were no audit rights at all under the procurement contract). As far as TML were concerned, one needs to remember that the 'contractor' actually comprised ten partner firms in all, with differing philosophies towards cost control and the analysis of cost data.

Contract negotiations have been described as 'uncompetitive', with Eurotunnel amendments standing little chance of getting through. Thus

> TML always believed that this project was theirs and that Eurotunnel was Johnny-come-lately, that Eurotunnel's role should be...to pay TML's monthly bills, give the nod on the design development, and no more than that. Anything more than that was perceived by TML as being ET interfering, ET being the shadow contractor (disputes panel member, interview, 1996).

That Eurotunnel was reluctant to play this role may be explained with reference to at least three factors. Firstly, the absence of any notion of project management within Eurotunnel at its inception was rectified with the establishment of the Project Implementation Division, albeit in March 1988, somewhat post-contract. Unfortunately, the capacity for this entity to exert any control over the project was frustrated by its initial inadequate staffing and opposition to it from TML, a reflection of the latter's general attitude towards Eurotunnel. The Project Implementation Division also effectively gave TML '[someone] to hit and to blame for everything that went wrong' (Eurotunnel legal team member, interview, 1996).

Secondly, there was the conflict over 'optimization', a concept fundamental to the Construction Contract, which referred to the achievement of the best balance between capital costs and operating costs. The problem in the Channel Tunnel project was that optimization was a very difficult concept to make operational because of the differing objectives and expectations that Eurotunnel and TML had and their 'total disagreement on how to interpret the term' (disputes panel member, interview, 1996). The view from within TML about the way in which the Construction Contract dealt with optimization supports this contention, with one interviewee stating that 'the relevant clauses were ambiguous, being the incoherent result of compromise reached during negotiations' (TML project manager 1, interview, 1996). Another (TML project manager 2, interview, 1996) considered that

> the concept of optimization did not allow for the fact that six months had already been knocked off an already tight project programme and during the CC [Construction Contract] negotiations. There was therefore little time left in an already overcrowded crucial front-end design phase for such a complex task, which would require the closest cooperation between the new operator and the contractor at the very time when a host of other priorities would be pressing for attention.

As far as the client asserting a more direct role was concerned this may be understood in terms of Eurotunnel's concerns about TML's view of optimization but also in terms of their agreement to the results of certain optimization studies (carried out by the contractor) being a requirement of the Construction Contract. Gradually, Eurotunnel realized that it would not be enough to leave the management of the Construction Contract to the Maitre d'Oeuvre organization, as was originally intended. Whilst its input remained important, Eurotunnel increasingly sought to ensure by more direct means that TML was not reducing its own capital costs by minimizing what they delivered, so raising Eurotunnel's maintenance costs (financial adviser to Eurotunnel, interview, 1996). The third factor, linked to both of the above, is that Eurotunnel was unhappy with the performance of TML and 'did not believe that they were doing everything they should be doing as quickly as they should be doing it and that [was particularly so] in the orders for the rolling stock' (financial adviser to Eurotunnel, interview, 1996). Here, it was considered that the contractors were primarily civil contractors, with skills in building not in the delivery of a complete rail transport system, rolling stock and all.

The way in which Eurotunnel and TML approached the resolution of disputes has been characterized as fitting what one member of the disputes panel refers to as the 'American approach'

> There were two camps within the project, neither of them...reckoned that...you sit down with other engineers and you sort out how to get on with things I think that the okay term nowadays is 'partnering'. [In] the American approach...you see a little bit of a problem coming and you immediately arm yourself with all the lawyers you can find and it is fought out on that basis. And the more lawyers appear on the scene, the more they persuade you that your case is strong and that's how to [resolve disputes]...(disputes panel member 2, interview, 1996).

The adversarial nature of contractual relations between Eurotunnel and TML, perhaps not surprisingly, may be said to stem from their different perspectives and objectives from the project, culminating in a 'winners and losers' mentality. However, the lack of a partnering approach has also been said to stem from personality clashes among the senior people at Eurotunnel and TML, partly linked to accusations of 'leaking' and misleading press briefings (Eurotunnel legal team member 2, interview, 1996). Further, there was a tendency to see the role of the disputes panel as being to resolve major disputes, with lower-order disputes being allowed to fester before being brought to the disputes panel. Indeed at the height of disagreements between Eurotunnel and TML, the remit and powers of the disputes panel became a matter for dispute, with both companies challenging rulings by the panel and pursuing the course of arbitration through the International Chamber of Commerce in Brussels, or additionally appealing to the High Court, the Court Appeal or the House of Lords. The powers of the Intergovernmental Commission embodied within the concession have also been criticized. Jack Lemley (Chief Executive of TML 1989-1993) has complained that the government's oversight body had 'free rein to change physical criteria without providing the money to do so' (Lemley, 1995). Indeed, Lemley adds, Eurotunnel could have been a tremendously rich utility had the IGC not taken away every margin for error. The IGC prioritized the safety of the system, and costly changes were imposed upon TML throughout the project. Lemley accuses the IGC of delays which caused modification costs to 'skyrocket' and considers that the concession agreement did not and could not provide for these unforeseen and costly changes. Haro Bedelian, Lemley's successor as Chief Executive at TML, also cites the avoidance of third parties (such as the IGC) with 'authority to change and control things but with no commensurate responsibility' as one of the lessons to be learnt from the Channel Tunnel project (Bedelian, 1995). In addition, Bedelian stresses the need for clearly defined roles for all parties involved in the project and, more specifically, the establishment of a strong client able to provide the contractor with definitive, timely operational information during design and to deal effectively with various third parties. The relevance of this may be appreciated when one considers the various organizational interfaces involved in coordinating design activity. Basically, TML had responsibility under the Construction Contract for drawing up initial outline designs. These were then to be passed to Eurotunnel, which in turn would pass them on to the IGC for approval, with both of the latter having consultations with the Maitre d'Oeuvre.

It is appropriate now to reflect on some of the main issues discussed in this section of the chapter. When the UK Government announced the intention to have such a large infrastructure project built by private means, and left the details to be determined in the course of competition, it placed the project on a unpredictable and uncoordinated route. In this regard Kirkland (Technical Director of Eurotunnel 1985-91) has stated the importance of having a means of coordinating the various reactions, objectives and values of the parties, and highlighted the problem of identifying the person or persons possessing the authority and vision to achieve this coordinating role (Kirkland, 1995). Perhaps the greatest problem arose from the nature of the organizational and contractual structures developed regarding the construction of the link, issues with implications for project definition and how it was to be realized and financed. As indicated earlier, many problems faced by the Channel Tunnel project can be traced back to the absence of an 'owner' in its formative months, since the bid for the fixed link scheme essentially was prepared and submitted by TML, under the guise of CTG, the 'owner/client' on the British side pre-Eurotunnel. Only the contractors and the banks mobilized the financial resources and technical expertise needed to prepare such a bid.

And while preparing the bid, the contractors had no interest in creating a client before they knew whether the bid had been successful. Post bid, it was in their interests to have a weak client (Kirkland, 1995).

Eurotunnel thus inherited a construction contract (and a contract already negotiated with BR and SNCF for the use of up to half of the tunnel's capacity) drawn up before its birth. Also, Eurotunnel accepted the terms of funding negotiated before it had acquired a 'mind of its own'. In this respect two additional comments may be made. First, the Terms Sheet, which formed the basis of the credit agreement by which the banks committed to finance the project was a 1500 page document that was close to being completed before Eurotunnel was formally incorporated and before its senior financial advisers were settled in post. As one interviewee recalls

> the Terms Sheet was all but complete on the 1st September [1986]. I was told that by the Friday of the week when I started [that] it had to be signed off because that was essential for the timetable for the publication of the Equity II prospectus. I barely had time to read it [and] make a few small changes. (Senior financial adviser, interview, 1996).

In addition to Eurotunnel's inability to influence the conditions of the Terms Sheet one might ask what role any assessment of risks played in Eurotunnel's acceptance of the terms of funding. Here, what is striking about assessments of constructions costs made in the run-up to the Equity II share issue, is the degree of concurrence between them. To some extent this must be set against a backdrop of the need to keep cost estimates down so as not deter potential investors. Nevertheless, the difference between estimates of construction cost made by TML, the banks' technical advisers and Eurotunnel was no more than £100 million out of a £2.8 billion prospectus figure. Thus, through the construction and loan agreements, TML and the banking consortium, the promoters of the project, were able to shift substantial risks onto Eurotunnel. It was not until 1990, when the project was in severe financial difficulties, that these risks were readdressed. And during this period the relationship between the contractors and Eurotunnel soured, the very opposite of what was required.

In summary, a key theme relating to this section concerns the view that an inflexible project such as the Channel Tunnel is likely to be promoted where processes of decision-making are centralized. The 'Invitation to Promoters' attracted many innovative alternatives to the provision of a fixed link, and the formal reason given for the rejection of these schemes was the lack of financial strength and proven technology. However, the account presented above indicates the influence of the CTG's powerful backers (the major banks and construction companies) on the Government, and the marginalization of key actors in the process concerning the scrutiny of the project, the design of the technology and related contractual arrangements. The British Government's insistence that the scheme be privately financed with no government subsidies appears to offer little support to the proposition that inflexible projects are highly centralized. Yet closer investigation reveals the extent of political guarantees and indirect financial support for the project either to facilitate the raising of funds or to enable the financing of important related projects connected to the eventual operation of the Channel Tunnel.

The clearest indicator of centralized decision-making, then, is the dominant position of the banking consortium and construction companies in setting up the Concession Agreement and its related contracts. Here, a decentralized decision-making process during the formation of the contracts may have benefited both the project and Eurotunnel, which was all but a 'missing actor' during the formation of the Concession Agreement and consequently was placed in a weak position relative to the other parties with which it was contracted. Indeed difficulties of coordination and mutual adjustment that have beset the project through the years owe much to the intractability of conflicts between Eurotunnel and TML and Eurotunnel and the banks, the seeds of which were sewn into contracts governing the project over which the client had little say. The next section aims evaluate the implications of these factors and the development of inflexible technology, as discussed in the previous section, for the financial performance of the project.

## Performance Evaluation

One of the guiding propositions of this book is that inflexible technology projects are expected to perform badly. The Eurotunnel project certainly appears to fit this assessment, at least in financial terms. Since late 1989 the project has constantly appeared in media headlines with details of its imminent collapse. Eurotunnel's cash flow now covers operating costs and marginal capital expenditure but, even with an agreement with banks to suspend required payments of its £700 million annual interest bill, prospects remain uncertain in the longer term. The Channel Tunnel project has characteristics typical of inflexible technological projects, with near to double the initially estimated capital costs expected (see Table 3.3) coupled with development slippage (Table 3.4). Here the proposed dates for reaching operational status are contrasted against the historical dates achieved.

**Table 3.4 Channel Tunnel project: development slippage**

| Planned delivery date | Historical delivery date | Months lost |
|---|---|---|
| 15 May, 1993 | 15 December, 1994 | 19 |

*Sources*: The 'planned' delivery date is cited in the November 1987 Eurotunnel prospectus, page 44 where it states 'The contractor is under general obligation to design, construct, test and commission a fully operational System for delivery by 15th May 1993.' The 'historical' date is taken from the Chairman's letter in the Eurotunnel annual report 1994 (Eurotunnel, 1995, page 5), where it states 'the management team...took Eurotunnel...to the fourth and final operating certificate, issued to us on 15 December 1994'. Although limited services were offered before this date, it is felt that the system was fully operational once all four services were commissioned.

In terms of the tunnelling technology employed the TBMs (on which performance was dependent) experienced early delays due to the prototype nature of the machines being used and their associated level of complexity (Robbins, 1995). This factor resulted in a late start and a long period of debugging, which jeopardized the financing and thus the viability of the whole project. However, once the debugging hurdle was overcome, the equipment proved highly successful as in 1990 and 1991; the tunnelling machines achieved monthly rates of advance of nearly double the original target rates. This progress was very fortunate as high rates of boring were required to make up for delays in the stages of tunnelling. The majority of the increase in cost appeared during the installation of the fixed equipment. The lump sum contract for the fixed equipment caused the most intractable problems with a claim 150% above the original sum agreed (Neerhout, 1994). In July 1989, it emerged that Eurotunnel's £6 billion funding package would be insufficient to complete the job. At that time, Eurotunnel blamed the contractors for the increased cost and estimated final costs to be £7 billion. TML responded by blaming increased costs on changes Eurotunnel had made in the project's specification and proposed the final cost to be closer to £7.5 billion (1990 prices). As mentioned above, the difference was mostly accounted for by a claim for £380 million made by TML against Eurotunnel for changes in the construction of the terminals and the mechanical and electrical works for the tunnels. This placed

Eurotunnel in default of its loan agreement as Eurotunnel had to have enough money in place at all times throughout the project to complete the link.

In 1990, financial difficulties and the prospect of defaulted loans prompted the banks to negotiate for a better balance of risks although, as Marcou (1993) notes, the renegotiated terms were not especially hard on the construction companies. With Eurotunnel technically in breach of the loan agreement, the banks were placed in a powerful position over the project. A refinancing agreement at the end of 1990 highlights further governmental assistance to the troubled project. In 1990, a further £2.7 billion of equity and loan finance had to be raised. At the time of refinancing the service tunnel had broken through, but more importantly the UK Government had rejected a request by the Eurorail consortium for the public funding and guarantees of a British rail link. The Japanese, who provided 23% of the debt in the 1987 financing, viewed this as a lack of support and thus threatened Eurotunnel's attempt to raise the further finance needed. This was resolved only after direct intervention by Mrs Thatcher in a letter to the Japanese Prime Minister, reaffirming the Government's commitment to the Channel Tunnel project (Vickerman, 1994). Furthermore, finance provided by European institutions could be considered to provide another method of indirect governmental assistance. The European Investment Bank provided a £1.3 billion loan along with the European Coal and Steel Community providing a £200 million loan on 'favourable terms'. A further form of indirect subsidy comprises the revenue Eurotunnel will receive from the railways in the form of tolls for every passenger and tonne of freight carried.

How should performance be determined, ultimately? Some may suggest the delivery of a complex major European transport system within a year of the date fixed at its inception compares favourably compared to other infrastructure systems. Doubtless the Channel Tunnel represents a major engineering achievement directly linking the UK with the European mainland for the first time. It clearly provides a service to millions of cross-Channel travellers and some spin-off benefits (and costs) to Kent and South-East England. However, the project economics tells another story of the performance of the investment - especially in the light of the project's near collapse due to financing costs. In the paragraphs below the Channel Tunnel's performance is assessed in terms of: a) the cost of building the tunnel, mostly capital costs; and b) the revenue gained from the traffic passing through the tunnel once it is operational.

With the financing costs on the debt amounting to approximately £700 million per year, Eurotunnel desperately needed quick, substantial and sustained positive cash flows. The traffic passing through the tunnel therefore is a critical component in maintaining Eurotunnel's existence. However, in addition to underestimating capital costs and lead times, traffic and revenues generated have been overestimated. The build-up of traffic and new services through the tunnel have been delayed, affected in part by the fire in 1996, and revenues per passenger have been slashed by a price war with the ferries. A forecast of 6 million passengers in 1995 has been reduced to 4 million, and then again to 2.5 million (*Financial Times*, 1998). Freight traffic has also been lower than forecast (*The Independent*, 1995).

The Channel Tunnel project supports the proposition that inflexible technology projects perform badly. Table 3.5 estimates the net present value of the tunnel scheme using discounted cash flow analysis. Although the Channel Tunnel is privately financed which usually justifies the adoption of a 25% plus discount rate in assessing investment opportunities, this analysis employs a favourably low 15% discount rate. A 15% rate is closer to the standard test discount rate adopted by public sector organizations in similar infrastructure schemes and is used in an attempt to provide the private decision makers the benefit of the doubt and a large degree of 'slack'. If the cost and revenue assumptions stated in the 1987 prospectus had turned out to be correct, the project would have had a positive net present value and a return on investment of 16.2% (see scenario 'A'). However, the question remains 'is this an acceptable figure and does it justify investment from the markets?' During the Equity II share issue, it became clear that insurance companies, pension funds and other institutions were distinctly unimpressed with the expected rate of return. Indeed, stockbrokers Phillips and Drew issued a research paper entitled 'Digging Deep for Eurotunnel', which questioned whether the modest return was worth the risk. It stated that 'even if the base case assumptions are right, these returns are low by venture capital standards and indeed are below the UK industrial average in the last ten years' (Jones, 1987). Thus, a 16.2% return was considered poor, considering the risks and required capital investment involved.

Scenario 'B' is again based upon the 1987 Prospectus, and aims to highlight the effect on return that an incorrect estimation of revenues may have had. A reduction in sales revenues from the forecast level, along the lines of those suffered by Eurotunnel in the first three years of the operation of the tunnel's services, greatly reduces the rate of return, producing a negative net present value using a 15% discount rate. Scenario 'C' calculates the rate of return based upon revenues remaining the same as those projected in 1987, but construction costs values being that which actually occurred. Again, returns are reduced to a less acceptable 14.3%. Scenario 'D' shows the large increase (72%) in revenues required to gain a more acceptable 25% rate of return.

**Table 3.5 Net present values and rates of return for The Channel Tunnel project (various scenarios)**

| Scenario | NPV £m (rounded) | Rate of return % |
|---|---|---|
| A 1987 prospectus figures | 1000 | 16.2 |
| B 1987 prospectus figures: sales revenue –50% | -4510 | 9.1 |
| C 1987 prospectus revenue figures, 1994 capital costs | -720 | 14.3 |
| D 1987 prospectus figures: sales revenue +72% | 8950 | 25.0 |
| E 1987 prospectus figures: sales revenue +10% | 1540 | 17.4 |
| F 1987 prospectus figures: sales revenue –10% | -70 | 14.9 |
| G 1994 Rights Issue figures | -5790 | 8.0 |
| H 1994 Rights Issue figures: sales rev. +10% | -5180 | 8.9 |
| I 1994 Rights Issue figures: sales revenue – 10% | 6410 | 7.1 |
| J 1994 Rights Issue revenue figures, 1987 construction cost estimate | -5240 | 8.3 |

*Sources*: Calculations for scenarios made by author based on data in the Eurotunnel Prospectus, 1987 and the Eurotunnel Rights Issue, 1994 document, cash flows discounted at 15% per annum.

The second half of Table 5 (scenario 'G' onwards) is based upon the 1994 rights issue document and provides a clearer picture of the actual rate of return expected to be seen on the project. At this point it should be noted that Eurotunnel has been experiencing difficulties in reaching these revenue figures and thus even these figures may be optimistic. Scenario 'G' shows an 8% expected rate of return and a negative net present value figure. This figure may be compared with those produced on scenarios 'H' and 'I', which highlight the small effect of revenue changes on the rate of return. Finally scenario 'J' indicates that even if the tunnel did reach its construction cost targets, reduced revenues would still adversely affect the rate of return.

## Conclusions

The Channel Tunnel project is highly inflexible. The high capital intensity of the project indicates the difficulty of reversing the investment decision, owing to the sunk costs involved and the sense of mission connected with the project. The Channel Tunnel, despite being a major engineering achievement and European infrastructure system, possesses the hallmarks of an inflexible project, as referred to in proposition (i), above. In terms of expected returns on investment, the project appears to be heading towards being a costly failure, unless such performance is considered on the basis of relatively optimistic scenarios and benign discount rates. Indeed, the 1995 Eurotunnel Progress Report states that during its negotiations with the banks over the restructuring of Eurotunnel's debts, the Group informed the banks that no assumptions should be made about the repayment of principal plus interest out of cash flows earned over the life of the Concession Agreement (Eurotunnel, 1995b). In 2000, Eurotunnel remains chronically overburdened with debt and unable service it merely by trading its way out (despite achieving market share of 54% of cross-channel passenger, and 39% of cross-channel freight traffic in 1999). Some measure of respite has been given by a financial restructuring agreement reducing interest charges by about 40%, with the banks' share of equity in Eurotunnel rising to 45%. The deal has enabled Eurotunnel to apply exceptional items retrospectively to its accounts, converting underlying losses (operating profit less interest) into net profits. In 1998, this resulted in an underlying of loss of nearly £200 million being converted into a net profit of £64 million. In 1999, an underlying loss of £139 million was converted into a net profit of £202 million, after allowing for an exceptional item of £296 million (Eurotunnel, 2000).

The inflexibility of the project was apparent from the early days, and ensured that many delays and costly mistakes occurred during its development and operation. In addition, the project exemplifies the concurrency warned against by Morris and Hough (1987). For example, the required speed of tunnelling work combined with uncertainty about the types of boring equipment that might be effective to ensure a coincidence of equipment testing and debugging with the need for that machinery to be in use. Another example of concurrency is the continued manufacture of specialized rolling stock, again to keep up with the project schedule, while there was still a possibility that costly safety-related design changes might be made (and indeed were made) by the IGC. Here, the relevant work, on doors on the shuttle trains, needed to be done again at extra expense and with lengthy delays to schedule. Generally, then, one might consider the paradoxical contribution of urgency and concurrency to delays in and the near-legendary cost overruns of Channel Tunnel development. Overall the finding of inflexibility leads to the reiteration of support for the view that large-scale technology projects can be expected to incur severe costs and be very difficult to develop. They thus compare unfavourably with an incremental approach, wherein the adoption of small changes and choices made in a way that emphasizes mutual adjustment better enable low cost trial-and-error learning.

The scale of the project exacerbated the problems of its organization, which has been much criticized and has contributed to poor financial performance. Here, the choice of the fixed link scheme and the organization of the concession were characterized by highly centralized decision-making. Yet in terms of the extent to which the promoters were able to shift the financial risks of the project onto the public purse, it would seem that there is little support for proposition (ii). After all, the project was financed without direct state funding or financial guarantees, although there was a certain amount that was borrowed from various European institutions. What is important to consider is the extent of political guarantees to would-be lenders, and the public financing of related infrastructure such as the TGV Nord rail link in France, without which the operation of the completed tunnel would be impaired. The governments of Britain and France thus played a pivotal role in ensuring that the momentum of the project would be maintained. In addition, the lobbying of financial institutions by the Bank of England to encourage them to participate in the key share issues and loans that generated financing for the project, further exemplifies the indirect involvement of public organizations in funding. Moreover, in the event that Eurotunnel is ever made bankrupt, Holliday speculates on public policy options, considering that simply not operating the tunnel or transferring operational responsibility to another concessionaire are non-starters, leaving the third option, which would be to rescue the scheme with public funds (Holliday, 1989). So, while acknowledging that the scheme has been financed primarily through the private sector, the proposition that inflexible technology is associated with centralized choice holds.

Support for proposition (ii) is strengthened when the role of the scheme's powerful promoters is recognized. It is clear from the above that the promoters of the project, the banks and the construction companies, dominated the negotiation of the related contracts, a process that does not seem to have been conducted on the basis of concern with the long-term economics of the project *per se*. Indeed, Stannard (1990) notes that the contractors were interested in acquiring building work, the banks were interested in the margins they could earn from lending, and others such as merchant bankers, lawyers and technical consultants had their own pecuniary interests in the project. However, none of these parties wanted to own and operate the project. As a result, the client and owner, Eurotunnel, was a missing actor and had little influence in the formation of the contracts and for a while in subsequent affairs. This situation did little to facilitate the management of project technology, related to the specification and conduct of design and construction, or to nurture a more collaborative approach to project management between the contractor and the eventual operator of the Channel Tunnel.

It is important to set the abrasive relationship between Eurotunnel and TML in the context of the 'polo mint' structure existing at the start of the project and thus the various key decisions taken by the promoters over which Eurotunnel had little influence. As well as representing areas where the owner had little initial access to decision-making they also reflect subsequent difficulties connected to the renegotiation of contracts, making changes to design and the reallocation of risks among the parties. For example, in order to meet the deadline set for the completion of construction in the concession and also to make financing a more attractive proposition, the promoters decided on a tight seven-year design and construction period. Further, an optimistic and premature view of the required technology pervaded the specification of the construction period and contractual mechanisms such as the lump sum arrangement for the mechanical and electrical work. Contracting and design were 'out of phase' with each other. The banks tended to regard the prices quoted for elements of work as being fixed despite the fact that there were many design and other uncertainties to be confronted once the project was underway. The contractor needed to bid low in order to win the design and build contract, in advance of the owner's (or the safety authority's) specification of design. Different interpretations of design were translated into bitter conflicts over 'optimization'. In this regard, early commitment to a particular design was deceptive and disadvantageous since the absence of the operator's input (remembering Eurotunnel's design obligation under the concession) and the general technological uncertainties yet to be resolved indicate the implausibility of considering design to be 'frozen' in this way (c.f. Morris and Hough, 1987 advice on early agreement and freezing of design). Concerned with the amount of risk to which they would be exposed, the banks' negotiators insisted on a single design-and-build construction contract in which the contractor became the focus of responsibility for all aspects of the work, rather than an arrangement where separate contracts were struck for different areas of the project (which seems to have been the preferred option within Eurotunnel).

With particular regard to rolling stock procurement where TML's member companies had little experience, this particular move frustrated any capacity for the owner to adopt a 'horses for courses' approach to contracting for various activities, according to the expertise of the bidding contractor. It could be argued that there was a great deal of debate between various organizations during the course of Channel Tunnel development (and indeed in operation bearing in mind recent discussions between Eurotunnel and the financing banks), which would detract from the centralization thesis at issue here. However, it should be borne in mind that an incremental approach emphasizes the involvement and compromise of actors potentially to be affected by decision-making. In this case a major player, Eurotunnel, did not have a seat at the table at which decisions that were to impose severe costs on the company were taken. Also, to some extent public scrutiny was short-circuited by the adoption of a hybrid Bill for ratifying the Treaty of Canterbury. Action to reallocate the risks of the project, and involving a more central role for the client in the discussions, did follow subsequently, but at the outset the incremental thesis was breached: at least one very significant stakeholder was marginalized from the policy making process. In addition, over the course of development, interaction between key protagonists can hardly be said to proceed on the basis of mutual adjustment, or a 'partnering' approach to the project.

Finally, it is necessary to address the matter of what an incremental approach has to offer by way of an alternative vision of decision-making regarding the Channel Tunnel project. Hypothetically, an alternative incremental approach would involve relatively small-scale investments in a range of European transport projects. Improvements in existing rail, sea or air provision would be the focus of such a process. Decision making under such an approach is dispersed across the various parties: companies/owners operating in the different segments of the transport industry, but having a (pecuniary) interest in both development and operational aspects of any particular scheme; the 'market', in the sense of considerations of market demand for and the use of proposed infrastructure, and the normal workings of investment appraisal by would-be funding institutions free of undue influence to invest from governmental agencies; and the diverse communities represented in local, national or regional planning processes for each scheme. Compared with a project such as the Channel Tunnel, such investments would be arguably less demanding of specialized technology required for safety reasons, for example. Furthermore, unglamorous incremental investments would not be the subject of the extraordinary sense of mission and the momentum that seems to characterize large-scale mega-projects. This means that any work on novel technical design that needs to be carried out may be conducted in a manner consistent with the avoidance of concurrency. In addition, the eventual application of design to manufacture or construction will be to relatively small units (for example, to individual ferries rather than to whole fleets which must need to be in service at a predetermined and rapidly approaching deadline). In this way, the potential costs of subsequent design changes may be kept low since modifications may be applied progressively to different units on the basis of efficient trial and error learning and operational experience. On this basis proposition (iii) regarding the availability of a more flexible option is supported. The key issues at stake in this chapter are taken up once more in the following chapter, which presents the case of wave power research and development in the UK.

## References

Anderson, G., and Roskrow, B. (1994), *The Channel Tunnel Story*, E and FN Spon, London.

Bedelian, H. (1995), 'Lessons from a Major BOT (Build, Own, Transfer) Project: the Channel Tunnel', *Transcript of a presentation to Portsmouth University*, Portsmouth, 15 June 1995.

Benard, A., and Morton, A. (1989), 'The Private Sector Financing of the Channel Tunnel', in Institution of Civil Engineers, *The Channel Tunnel*, Thomas Telford, London.

DETR (Department of Environment, Transport and the Regions) (2000), *Press Briefing*, no. 407, 8 June.

Eurotunnel (1987), *Eurotunnel Prospectus*, Eurotunnel, London and Paris.

Eurotunnel (1990), *Eurotunnel Rights Issue*, Eurotunnel, London and Paris.

Eurotunnel (1994), *Eurotunnel Rights Issue*, Eurotunnel, London and Paris.

Eurotunnel (1995a), *Annual Report, 1994*, Eurotunnel, London and Paris.

Eurotunnel (1995b), *Progress Report*, Eurotunnel, London and Paris.

Eurotunnel (2000), *Annual Report, 1999*, Eurotunnel, London and Paris.

*Financial Times* (1998), 17 February.

Fisher, J. (1993), 'Industrial Relations and the Construction of the Channel Tunnel', *Industrial Relations Journal*, vol. 24, pp. 211-225.

Holliday, I. (1989), *Privatizing Transport Infrastructure: The Politics of Channel Tunnel Concession*, The Channel Tunnel Research Unit, University of Kent.

*The Independent* (1989), 26 May.

*The Independent* (1995), 15 September.

Jones, B. (1987), *The Tunnel, The Channel and Beyond*, Ellis Horwood, London.

Kirkland, C. (1995), 'The Channel Tunnel - lessons learned', *Tunnelling and Underground Space Technology*, vol. 10, pp. 5-6.

Lemley, J. (1995), 'Managing the Channel Tunnel - Lessons Learned', *Tunnelling and Underground Space Technology*, vol. 10, pp. 9-11.

Marcou, G. (1993), 'Public and Private Sectors in the Delivery of Public Infrastructure: the Case of the Channel Tunnel from an International Perspective', *Environment and Planning C: Government and Policy* vol. 11, pp.1-18.

Morris, P.W.G., and Hough, G.H. (1987), *The Anatomy of Major Projects: A Study of the Reality of Project Management*, Wiley, Chichester.

Morton, A. (1995a), *Transcript of Speech to EC Banks in the City*, London, 20 October.

Morton, A. (1995b), 'In-built Conflicts Resolved at a Price', *International Railway Journal*, May, pp. 10-11.

Neerhout, J. (1994), cited in: Fairweather, V., The Channel Tunnel: Larger than Life, and Late, *Civil Engineering*, May, pp. 42-46.

Ratzer, P. (1995), 'Lessons from Eurotunnel', *Project Finance International*, vol. 70, pp. 28-29.

Robbins, R. (1995), 'Boring Under the Channel: one perspective on the experience', *Tunnelling and Underground Space Technology*, vol. 10, pp. 23-25.

Stannard, C.J. (1990), 'Managing a mega-project - the Channel Tunnel', *Long Range Planning*, vol. 23, pp. 49-62.

Vickerman, R. (1989), *The Private Provision of Infrastructure: The Channel Tunnel Project*, The Channel Tunnel Research Unit, University of Kent.

Vickerman, R. (1991), *Financing the Channel Tunnel*, The Channel Tunnel Research Unit, University of Kent.

Vickerman, R. (1994), *The Channel Tunnel: The Case for Private Sector Provision of Public Infrastructure?* The Channel Tunnel Research Unit, Kent University.

# 4 Wave Power

## Introduction

The need for more environmentally benign energy remains a potent policy issue. Offshore wave energy is a potentially abundant and environmentally safe source of electricity supply for the UK. Moreover, the UK once led the way in terms of learning about the resource and the technical means by which its riches might be cost-effectively captured. In 1982, however, amid a great deal of controversy, the UK offshore wave energy programme was virtually closed down, without the demonstration of an operational prototype, though this has been the subject of periodical governmental review. The case of the research, development and demonstration (R,D&D) of wave power renewable energy technologies in the UK provides an opportunity for investigating the socio-political construction of technology. This chapter thus continues the work of the book by analyzing the case of a technology that was considered by UK policy makers to be proceeding successfully only to fall behind other renewable energy sources in terms of central funding, technical development, and capacity supplied. As in previous chapters the concern is to highlight the social and political processes that have promoted or hindered technology development, in conjunction with considerations of the machinations involved in assessing the state of technology development in an embryonic sector such as wave power.

By considering the development of wave power in the UK, it will be possible to identify factors that distort the construction process, so as to inhibit the deployment of potentially flexible, economic and democratic technological innovations, or to promote those which are risky, inflexible, and undemocratic. The next section of the chapter evaluates the extent to which wave energy development projects supported by UK policy makers in the 1970s and early 1980s could be characterized as 'inflexible'. Here, as before, the degree to which decision-makers are able to detect or correct errors, made in the development of technology, is key to understanding the notion of flexibility. A related and important set of issues concerns the organizational power and institutional contexts affecting the process of technology development, including the subjective nature of assessments of technological progress, operational and economic performance. Pertinent here are the implications for R,D&D of wave power technology of the monopoly of influence and information by certain actors, linked to the notion of non-decision making and the mobilization of bias. In particular, the third section of the chapter will build on the concept of technological momentum. An examination is made of the interplay between the market and political circumstances, the pace and scale of R,D&D activity and the facilitation of opportunities for learning about alternative technological means for exploiting wave energy resources. Relevant measures mooted in the proposed Utilities Regulation Bill are discussed. The final part of the chapter presents some theoretical and practical conclusions regarding the implications for the political and organizational management of technology development in emerging industry sectors. Of general concern are conditions under which learning about the potential performance of embryonic technologies might prosper and the indeterminate nature of evaluations about technical or economic performance. Such considerations refer to the scale and flexibility of technical alternatives, the nature of related socio-economic or political contexts, and the relationship of both of these sets of factors to the conduct and evaluation of R,D&D.

## Inflexibility and UK Wave Power

The following paragraphs examine research development and demonstration projects involving wave energy technology in the UK, in terms of the extent to which they may be characterized as 'inflexible', and also the degree to which they militate against low-cost trial-and-error experimentation and implementation. As in the two previous case studies the inflexibility of technology projects will be evaluated with reference to four indicators, which are restated below:

1. long lead time;
2. high capital intensity;
3. large unit size; and
4. dependence on specialized infrastructure.

Taking each factor in turn it is possible, initially at least, to establish the extent to which wave energy technology projects may be characterized as inflexible. Lead time refers to the time taken to research, design and construct wave energy facilities to the point at which a wave power station may be considered to be fully operational. As far as wave energy in the UK is concerned, the poverty of operational experience thus far means that estimates of lead times must be treated with extreme caution. Nevertheless, some indication of the lead times from R, D&D of wave power systems can be provided. An assessment of the economics and technical feasibility of wave power by the National Engineering Laboratory (1976), for example, put their 'best' estimate for the design and testing of components and models for a prototype as a period 'not exceeding three years'. Moreover, the NEL study saw it as being unlikely that a prototype of any system could be both researched and developed in a period of less than 5 years. A more dramatic estimate of the lead time has been given in connection with the development of a wave power station in Sweden (Lewis, 1985). This was rated at an installed capacity of 500 MW, was to consist of 25 000 buoys, produce 1 TWh annually and was envisaged to take about 25 years to complete.

As for the capital intensity of wave power, the following quotation by Grubb (1991) is worthy of consideration at the outset

> Only one generalization appears to apply to all renewable electricity sources, and that is that they are capital intensive, with relatively low operating costs.

Estimates of the operating and maintenance costs for wave energy systems vary widely, with no simple relationship applying to device size, as different device concepts have varying maintenance requirements. Nevertheless, point absorber systems have annual operating and maintenance values estimated at up to 6% of total capital costs, whereas systems fixed to the sea-bed (such as NEL's oscillating wave column) have values quoted at about 1% of total capital costs. The operating and maintenance costs of most devices assessed in the period under review (1970s and early-1980s) by the UK Department of Energy had quoted values of less than 2% of capital costs (Lewis, 1985). Similar values from other studies permitted some estimate of capital intensity to be made (Hagerman and Heller, 1988; Falnes and Lovseth, 1991). For example, Hagerman and Heller (1988) produced an analysis aimed at investigating the cost of energy from 12 wave energy plants in eight countries. The size of the plants varied from small (installed capacity of 0.35 MW) to large (2 GW). The load factors (or capacity factors) were between 13% and 60%, as estimated by the developers concerned. Zero inflation, a 30-year book life and a discount rate of 12.5% were also assumed. Capital expenditures ranged from US$580 per kW up to US$4830 per kW, and consisted of the developers' initial estimate, which was then indexed to the MARAD index of shipbuilding costs in the US, if possible (it was in eight of the 12 cases). The annual operating costs as a percentage of capital costs per kilowatt ranged from 0.4% to 7.9% per year, again as provided by developers. Based on the study made by Hagerman and Heller, the author has calculated the capital intensity of wave energy plants to range between 60% to over 95% of total costs. In particular, the two UK devices specifically identified in the Hagerman and Heller study ('Salter's Duck' and the 'SEA Clam') have been picked out. On the basis of this data, estimates of the capital intensity associated with these designs, together with other relevant data, have been produced (see Table 4.1). There is quite a disparity in capital intensity between the large-scale 'Duck' and the much smaller scale 'Clam' device, though in comparison to other projects and technological systems referred to in this book both designs look highly capital intensive.

Unit size provides the next aspect of the discussion of inflexibility. Here, it is interesting to consider the prospect of wave energy's potential contribution to electricity generation in the future. It is not unreasonable to suggest that wave energy could supply, say, one-fifth of the current level of UK electricity. Indeed, this figure falls between pessimistic estimates of one-sixth of the electricity supply and more optimistic views, putting the potential for wave energy's contribution at over one-third of UK electricity supply (Flood, 1991).

**Table 4.1 Capital intensity of selected UK wave energy devices**

| | Salter's Duck | SEA Clam |
|---|---|---|
| Plant size (MW installed) | 2000 | 2 |
| Capacity (load) factor (%) | 38 | 31 |
| Capital cost per kW (US $) | 1920 | 1040 |
| Annual operating cost (percentage of total capital cost, rounded) | 2 | 5 |
| Capital intensity (% rounded) | 90 | 70 |

* All costs have been discounted at a rate of 12.5% per annum using 1987 US dollars.

*Source*: Author's calculations based on data from Hagerman & Heller (1988).

To deliver the amount of electricity needed to satisfy this 2% target, i.e. approximately 60 TWh of electricity per year, the necessary installed capacity would have to be of the order of 25 GW (25 000 MW), assuming a load factor of 25% from the stations employed. The interesting thing about unit size relates to the ability for decision-makers to learn about and improve the performance of wave energy devices without undue costs being incurred. Indeed, more will be said on this matter below. For now, however, it is only necessary to note that an approach, such as that seemingly favoured by the Department of Energy in the late 1970s and early 1980s, would have resulted in the required installed capacity being met by only a few large-scale projects. Perhaps only a dozen or so stations with installed capacities of 2 GW each would need to be constructed. However, the more recent worldwide focus on smaller-scale stations might mean that the desired installed capacity could be met by, say, 100 stations with capacities of 250 MW, 250 stations with capacities of 100 MW, or even 25,000 stations with a capacity of 1 MW. Hence, initial UK policy towards R,D&D reveals a bias in favour of systems likely to have a large unit size.

On the matter of dependence upon a specialized infrastructure, a number of items are required for the viability of wave energy conversion systems to be ensured. These may be considered as aspects of design and construction, and power conversion and transmission activities. Such infrastructure needs have been shown to typify inflexible technology projects and may exacerbate problems stemming from other factors, such as long lead times or high capital intensities. As far as design and construction activities are concerned, infrastructure requirements may be identified in the construction, mooring and anchoring of wave energy structures. For a large-scale system, such as the hypothetical station of capacity 2 GW used as a basis for evaluating wave energy devices by the Energy Technology Support Unit (ETSU), specialized infrastructure needs would be very significant. In a manner redolent of experience with North Sea oil development in the 1960s and 1970s, the ETSU suggested that the construction of the modules for such a station would require mass production techniques on a scale 'not previously known in the concrete industry' (Department of Energy, 1985). This is not a surprising view, bearing in mind that a typical station might involve several units, each weighing over 20,000 tonnes. The scale of such an effort is underlined by the declaration that concrete production for a single wave energy station of capacity 2 GW would represent about 5% of total annual production in the UK. As for the nature of construction sites, in particular, a station of capacity 2 GW might typically require a site covering an area of 120 hectares. Then, facilities would need to include a concrete-casting factory capable of mass production of pre-cast units; an area for the assembly of the device and other equipment; a launching area in the form of either a shipway or ship lift; and appropriate mechanical machinery for moving heavy structures and equipment (Department of Energy, 1985).

Mooring and anchoring are critical to the safety and survival of wave energy devices, whether the device floats or is attached to the sea-bed in some way. The inadequacy of existing technical approaches to mooring system design for large-scale offshore wave energy systems has been recognized. In particular, a number of factors may be identified which render traditional solutions unsuitable. These include the location of wave power stations in water depths of up to 100 m and the large number of structures within a system that would need to be installed. Further considerations are the permanence of the moorings, which would put reliability at greater issue, and the nature of the sea-bed at station sites, i.e. it being hard rock with little silt or sediment covering it. A final point relates to the compliance versus stiffness question, with offshore wave energy systems requiring mooring of greater compliance than that which conventional anchor and chain systems used on ships have provided. Among some of the innovations that have attempted to address this issue are tension leg mooring, single-point and multi-point mooring systems, drilled pile rock anchors and dead-weight anchors.

Dependence upon specialized infrastructure can again be identified for power conversion and transmission aspects of wave energy systems. Essentially, wave energy needs to be converted into a suitable form of energy (usually electricity) if it is to be practically transmitted to consumers. Efforts to improve conversion efficiency to levels acceptable by the developers of the 'Salter Duck', for example, have necessitated the design of new types of hydraulic machinery and of new kinds of bearing, which could work only in water. Furthermore, a high-speed, variable pump/motor was developed to drive the generator and to facilitate energy storage (Salter, 1989).

### *Inflexibility and the Correction of Error*

Offshore wave power systems appear to possess all the hallmarks of inflexible technology projects. Although the information available must be treated with great care, lead times appear to be long, capital intensity high, unit sizes large and a great deal of specialized infrastructure would be required for the effective installation. The combination of these factors means that, should such systems as the hypothetical ETSU reference stations actually have been implemented, the cost of correcting any errors made would have been very high. Essentially, enormous investments of time, capital and other resources would have to have been made before any learning about actual performance and improvements of the systems could be realized. Such learning might be in the form of an improved understanding of the efficiency of energy conversion, of project management coordination or of the storage and transmission of converted energy, for example. The central problem is that any learning in areas such as these could only be obtained after the initial commitment of substantial resources. Hence, the original investment decision, in effect, would not be reversible or corrigible, except at great cost or loss of face. This would mean severe restrictions on the decision-makers' subsequent freedom to manoeuvre; a high price to pay in any decision-making situation.

However, there is more to this than apparently first meets the eye. As Grubb (1990) notes, 'technology is never static'. Indeed, one of the major factors inhibiting the progress of renewable energy sources has been the 'analytic conservatism' inherent in the evaluation and projection of the development of embryonic technology (Grubb, 1990). Rather undue pessimism regarding the future progress of wave energy systems is reflected in bodies such as the ETSU basing their analyses on large-scale systems, featuring long lead times, *inter alia*. Hence, it is not surprising that the kinds of system evaluated turned out to be very demanding of resources, inflexible and thus potentially uneconomic. This and other institutional- or market-related aspects of the distortion of the process and evaluation of research and development in UK wave energy are considered in the following section.

## Momentum and the Context of R,D&D Decisions

The main objective of this section is to try to explain the progress of UK wave energy R,D&D, in terms of the socio-political factors affecting it. Aspects of what follows concern the role of socio-political actors in developing a sense of mission or technological momentum, or in creating bias in the process of the construction of technology. As above, relevant issues involve the extent to which the process of decision-making has been centralized, such that interested or potentially affected parties have been marginalized. The role of government and quasi-governmental institutions, and mechanisms for evaluating prospective R,D&D projects also come under scrutiny.

The concept of momentum applied to the evolution of technologies may be used to explain the manner in which a technological system appears to develop an energy of its own, so that it attracts the scientists, technicians, capital and administrators that it needs to become established (Hughes,

1983; 1987). In this case study, the interplay between momentum and the flexibility of large technological systems is a source of interest. More specifically, attention is directed toward the relationship between a sense of supraordinate mission, technological momentum, the apparent inflexibility of wave energy systems and to the adoption of low-cost, trial-and-error approaches to R,D&D. The momentum of UK wave energy R,D&D may be described as uneven, bringing to mind Hughes' notion of reverse salients, which is suggestive of evolving technological systems where some components become 'out of phase' with others. Such situations can have the effect of limiting the potential of the developing technological system. Flood (1991) points to the unevenness of the momentum of the UK wave power programme as follows:

> The wave energy programme ... was directed towards designing a massive 2000 MW 'Reference Design' wave energy station notionally sited off the West coast of Scotland a task that can be likened to designing a supertanker whilst at the same time developing the principles of naval architecture.

Other aspects of the programme, which characterize unevenness, may be identified. These include a shortage of funds for testing and trials, closed decision-making processes, unduly pessimistic cost and reliability assumptions, and costing techniques that favoured low weight rather than high flexibility innovations. These factors were interrelated and affected the prospects for progressive, experiential learning about possible smaller-scale or more flexible technical approaches to the development of wave energy systems.

One illustration of the poverty of funding for wave energy R,D&D even before the cessation of public funding for offshore devices in 1982 relates to the asymmetry of the Department of Energy's allocations between the renewable energy and nuclear energy sectors. By 1982, total spending on all research for renewables was only - 15 million (nominal terms). This compared very unfavourably with over £200 million per year that was being spent on the nuclear power research programme and the size of the renewables budget in other major industrialized countries at the time (see Tables 4.2 and 4.3; Jeffrey, 1990; Flood, 1982). (In 1996, the UK ranked tenth among IEA countries for absolute expenditure on renewables, but nineteenth out of 24 in terms of the proportion of that expenditure to gross domestic product. Private plus Non-Fossil Fuel Obligation support for all renewables was estimated at approximately £3-400 million in 1998/99 (DTI, 1999a).) The comparison between nuclear power and wave energy expenditure in particular is all the more striking considering Salter's modest estimate for the cost of research on the Duck device of £0.25 million per year (Flood, 1982). One explanation for the shortage and eventual stoppage of central funding of offshore wave energy research has been cited as the need for the Department of Energy to trim its renewable energy budget by £3 million in 1982 (Jeffrey, 1990). Another explanation refers to the centralization of decision-making concerning such research and the influence of institutions being biased towards the cause of nuclear power and against renewables, in general, but wave energy in particular. Jeffrey (1990: 85) is especially scathing on this matter, offering the view that the lack of support given to renewables research and development in the UK

> can only be understood in the light of the determination of the nuclear lobby to press on with Britain's nuclear programme at any cost, in spite of considerable public opposition. If benign renewable sources could be demonstrated as viable alternatives ... then Britain's plans to expand nuclear power would collapse.

**Table 4.2 Government expenditure on R&D in the renewable and nuclear energy sectors (1979-1992 £million, 1992 terms)**

| Year | Renewables | Nuclear |
|---|---|---|
| 1979-80 | 19 | 345 |
| 1980-81 | 23 | 376 |
| 1981-82 | 27 | 364 |
| 1982-83 | 21 | 354 |
| 1983-84 | 19 | 325 |
| 1984-85 | 23 | 299 |
| 1985-86 | 20 | 273 |
| 1986-87 | 17 | 222 |
| 1987-88 | 21 | 186 |
| 1988-89 | 20 | 196 |
| 1989-90 | 21 | 158 |
| 1990-91 | 22 | 142 |
| 1991-92 | 24 | 93 |

*Source*: Hansard, House of Commons Energy Committee (1992).

Referring more directly to the demise of the offshore wave power progamme, Jeffrey (1990: 85) offers this explanation.

> In 1976, the Department of Energy ... believed that wave power was 'the most attractive of the renewables sources' while wind power was seen as being

> much less viable. It was therefore in the interests of the nuclear industry to boost wind power as a 'winner' ... and run down the prospects of wave power.

The lack of a genuine voice to represent the interests of renewable energy is another significant aspect of the decline in support for wave power R,D&D. Hence, the location of responsibility for renewables research at the ETSU, administered by the UK Atomic Energy Authority and based at the UK's main research centre at Harwell, has been seen as 'disingenuous' (Flood et al, 1982)

> staff are bound to be influenced by the prevailing ethos of the establishment within which they operate, and the Atomic Energy Research Establishment can hardly be described as neutral in any debate on energy.

**Table 4.3 Government R&D budgets for renewable energy in IEA countries (millions of 1990 US dollars)**

| Country | 1981 | % energy budget | 1990 | % energy budget |
|---|---|---|---|---|
| Canada | 82 | 17 | 13 | 4 |
| Denmark | 6 | 20 | 9 | 22 |
| W. Germany | 114 | 7 | 105 | 20 |
| Italy | 62 | 6 | 56 | 7 |
| Japan | 157 | 61 | 96 | 4 |
| Netherlands | 32 | 14 | 22 | 14 |
| Spain | 34 | 23 | 8 | 13 |
| Sweden | 89 | 31 | 19 | 19 |
| UK | 48 | 6 | 29 | 10 |
| USA | 934 | 20 | 113 | 4 |
| IEA Total | 1661 | 13 | 526 | 7 |

*Source*: IEA 1990 review.

In view of this unfortunate alignment, it is not surprising that Friends of the Earth, among others, called for a separate renewables agency to coordinate the various activities involved in renewables R,D&D, and for new national laboratories and testing centres for individual renewable energy sources. The centralization issue must also refer to the question of access to, and understanding and dissemination of information on the part of relevant factors a matter that is linked to their technical capabilities and psychological orientation. Each factor has contributed to the rather uneven momentum of UK wave energy R,D&D by distorting the evaluation of technical and commercial progress in the sector and the prospects for future public or privately sourced funding.

For the developers involved in the wave energy sector, inertia, misunderstanding and secrecy were typical of their dealings with research programme managers in the ETSU. Wave energy researchers have complained that much of the administrative machinery seemed to have been designed to 'delay and demoralize', rather than with the aim of facilitating research and development. Moreover, the view has been expressed by researchers that ETSU project officers did not understand the technology, did not want to understand it and thus were unable to represent the views of the device teams (Flood et al, 1982). To make matters worse, the meeting of ACORD (the Department of Energy's Advisory Council on Research and Development) on 19 March 1982 saw the exclusion of Clive Grove-Palmer, programme manager for wave energy, and also the programme managers for other renewable sources. It was this meeting that considered a secret report that the wave energy teams were not allowed to see for another eight months; a report that recommended that future departmental funding should be run down, owing to wave-power's lack of economic attractiveness (Jeffery, 1990).

The unevenness of momentum that has been central to the discussion so far is further characterized by much of the debate concerning the economics of wave energy. There has been a continuing controversy concerning various estimates of device reliability and the unit costs per kilowatt-hour of different wave energy systems. Of particular significance here is the undue pessimism of the assumptions made in arriving at cost estimates contained in the ETSU and ACORD reports of the 1980s. For example, in 1982, ACORD produced an estimate for the cost of electricity for the Salter Duck of 9.8 pence per kWh, based on an assumed load factor of 20%. It was following this that departmental support was removed from the offshore wave programme. In 1990, this figure was finally withdrawn, after considerable pressure from the wave lobby, and a new estimate of 5.2p per kWh was produced, based on a new availability factor of 38%, immediately making the Duck much more attractive. In the intervening period, according to Salter, 'bankruptcy loomed close' (House of Commons Energy Committee, 1992, paragraph 54).

In connection with this the Energy Committee of the House of Commons (1992, paragraph 55) notes 'with regret' that

> in the case of wave power, instead of continuing ... R&D in order to reduce the uncertainty, the Department of Energy withdrew all funding on the ground of assumptions which it knew had been, in the words of one official, 'picked from the air'. We consider that, in the past, the Department has attempted to establish costs at too early a stage in a technology's development; to draw final conclusions from tentative assessments; and placed too little value on the continuity of funding. It is difficult to regard the history of renewable R&D funding in the UK as other than a history of volte-faces, premature judgements and plain errors.

If the timing of the assessment of embryonic technology is critical to the perceptions of potential performance and the momentum necessary for the continuation of the process of R,D&D, then so too is the method of evaluation undertaken. Thus, the use of discounted cash flow techniques for the appraisal of renewables became a prime source of concern (Elliott, 1992; House of Commons Energy Committee, 1992; Smith, 1991). To advocates of renewable energy discounted cash flow analysis is an approach that encourages short-termism and unfairly penalizes investments with potentially large benefits into the very long term, depending on the required rate of return and payback period. This problem is highlighted by increases in the norm for public sector required rates of return. In addition, in the privatized environment of the electricity supply industry, investments would be likely to be subject to discount rates of between 10% and 15% or more and also to shorter-term project contracts.

Moreover, a continuing problem has been the comparison of renewables with fossil fuel and nuclear energy generation, in terms of the need to account for their respective environmental costs and benefits. It has already mentioned that, as well as being abundant, wave energy has the great attraction of being potentially the most benign source of renewable energy in terms of its likely environmental impact. However, its potential has and continues to be disadvantaged by the uncertainties and difficulties involved not only calculating external costs but in defining what even constitutes an externality. To reiterate, this sort of problem has served only to distort the potential attractiveness of wave energy systems, leading to the eventual demise of the R,D&D effort in the offshore arena.

Finally, the construction of flexible systems to exploit wave power will not be helped by the poverty of mechanisms for relating the R,D&D process to the potential markets to be served. This is especially relevant to the task of eventually progressing from the research stage of the development of wave energy systems to their commercial deployment. Government policy is a particularly important aspect of this process, given that wave energy technologies will have to compete with established energy sources and also other renewables, such as wind power, which are close to commercial deployment. Here, the absence of schemes for the demonstration of operational prototypes has not been helpful to the construction process. This has been reflective of a funding gap that has existed with respect to the latter stages of development work, necessary for the eventual commercialization of technology by industry. It has been suggested that demonstration schemes include generous allowances for the capital costs and monitoring costs of demonstrations, with industry increasingly bearing the risk as the innovation reaches the market (Flood, 1982). It would appear that demonstration was also hindered by the nature of the organization of government departments. Hence, prior to the absorption of the Department of Energy into the Department of Trade and Industry in April 1992, industry participants complained of the UK's inability to fund major demonstration projects because of the 'compartmentalization of responsibilities' (House of Commons Energy Committee, 1984).

There has also been a lack of appropriate deployment targets or subsidies to stimulate investment in wave energy systems offshore, even now when the strategic importance of this energy source is no longer in doubt. The terms of the Non-Fossil Fuel Obligation (NFFO) and the Fossil Fuel Levy (both introduced under the 1988 Electricity Act) have had the intended effect of subsidizing nuclear power and providing a guaranteed market for the electricity that it produces. The arrangements have also adversely affected the market for renewables and the provision of sorely needed investment funds for R,D&D in the sector. Indeed, in 1990-91, the nuclear industry received over 98% of the proceeds generated from the levy on electricity sales (over £1.175 billion), with all the renewable energy sources together sharing the remainder. Furthermore, the renewables portion of the non-fossil fuel electricity that regional electricity companies in England and Wales are obliged to buy was set too low and, consequently, the 1990 and 1991 NFFOs were over-subscribed. Moreover, there has yet to be a specific tranche in the NFFO that would guarantee a market for wave energy; even if there were, present contractual arrangements would mean that projects would have to be economic over a period of about 6 years. Finally, the NFFO is primarily about large-scale electricity generation, not small-scale, remote or other projects producing heat or fresh water, for example. As such, policy arrangements have been unfavourable to those developments of wave energy with small-scale applicability, which may be more likely to become commercial in the near future than large-scale grid supply. Interestingly the proposal has been made that the NFFO in future should apply to renewable energy sources only and not nuclear power (DTI, 1999b). It would operate so as to reduce what have been significant barriers to investment, as discussed next.

*Contemporary Developments*

As time has progressed, and with the change of government in 1997, there seems to have been change of perspective in policy towards renewables. Wave power though apparently continues to suffer from the legacy of the experience of the 1970s and 1980s in that alone of the sources discussed at that time, it barely rates a mention in a recent government report on prospects for the development of renewable energy. A lack of commercial or demonstration schemes is given as an explanation for an inability to evaluate wave power's contribution to electricity generation (DTI, 1999a). While pondering on the extent to which this current perception of the failure of wave power is based on the distorted assessments of yesteryear, there is another interpretation of events. On this latter interpretation, whatever the rights and wrongs of previous policy, progress has been made over in terms of gradual learning about wave energy technology, with modest costs. For example, the small wave facility located on the coast of Islay has demonstrated the effectiveness of one type of design involving the oscillating water column and the Wells turbine. This 75 kW device obtained central funding to the tune of a modest £1.5 million and a new generation of devices now being developed 'draw heavily on the experience gained' from its operation. This includes a version of the turbine used at Islay applied to a larger but still relatively small-scale device, the 1 MW Osprey (DTI, 1999a).

The future prospects for both renewable energy in general and wave power in particular now appear to rest on the ability of government measures to ensure fairer competition between different sources of electricity supply, to encourage diversity of supply options and to reward flexible but dependable energy sources. From an incremental viewpoint the motivation underpinning this recent approach is interesting in that governmental commitment 'to put the environment at the heart of decision-making' has arguably more to do with eventually signing up to international climate change agreements to try to limit the potential damage associated with carbon emissions and greenhouse gases than any strong sense of purpose. Another ingredient shaping the policy context has been the progressive retreat of the State from central funding of energy R&D,

with the concomitant rise in the role of the market in investment, encouraged by a range of market stimulation measures. Thirdly, concerns about accidents and the decommissioning costs associated with nuclear power combined with growing public concern about its safety to produce a decline in commitment to that mode of generation. This was dramatically illustrated by the unwillingness of the market to subscribe.

One aspect of the fifth and largest Non-Fossil Fuel Obligation (1998) was the stimulation of the market for renewables by providing a guaranteed market and premium price for electricity supplied from renewable sources, subsidized by electricity consumers. A Green paper on proposals for a new framework regulating utilities in the UK sets out a number of measures connected to the opening up of the UK electricity generation and distribution market and the creation of a 'level playing field' between new, renewable and conventional sources of supply. Briefly, four areas may be outlined: the setting up of 'New Electricity Trading Arrangements' (NETA); the legal separation of electricity supply and distribution entities; the establishment of independent consumer councils in each utility sector; and 'transparency measures', to improve the clarity and legitimacy of the decision-making process (DTI, 1999b). The hoped-for benefits from such provisions, should they translate into legislation, are cited as the encouragement of new entrants, some of which will be more able to specialize successfully in market niches, and more as well as fairer competition, leading to ongoing reductions in the wholesale price of electricity. Against this is set the loss of the economies of scope available to the central generator of combining supply and distribution. Moreover, the approach appears to embody some 'bottom up' thinking in that consumers and embedded generators are subjects of the new framework's proposal. Consumers are described in terms of raising their ability to contribute to policy-making in the utilities sector, through being better informed about the implications of new programmes as they arise (DTI, 1999b). Also, local 'embedded' generators are promised to the focus of greater support so that community or non-grid suppliers can receive a fair price for their electricity (though this is partly to offset the costs of future government support for renewables developed in this way) (DTI, 1999a). Overall, the claim is made that such measures can provide greater transparency and certainty regarding the regulatory framework for utilities, with the effect of reducing the cost of capital of potential developers.

## Conclusions

This chapter has sought to characterize the nature of offshore wave energy technologies in the UK in terms of four factors, which together would indicate the extent of their inflexibility. It has discussed the construction of wave energy technology in terms of the social and political contextual factors which have affected R,D&D decisions in the area. In doing so the chapter has employed concepts from technology policy, political decision theory and the social construction of technology literature. A central theme has concerned the role that perceptions of the characteristics of wave energy technologies, interwoven with various social and institutional factors, have played in the unevenness of the momentum of wave energy R,D&D.

As Grubb (1990) observes, the problem with UK wave energy is not so much that there has not been momentum towards demonstrating an operational prototype; rather, the issue appears to be more one of stability and timing. A principal aim of policy and the research and development of emerging technologies must be to learn how they can be more flexibly and cost effectively deployed, but also to address more explicitly the political aspects of evaluations of technical operational performance. The demonstration of small-scale prototypes, or of the modularity of larger-scale systems, is a vital component of the process leading up to eventual deployment decisions. However, the case study has shown how the UK offshore wave energy programme was scuppered prematurely. It has been said that funding was perhaps 'too much, too fast', so the whole programme was cut because of disappointment with early results, or at least the perception of poor progress. Whatever the validity of this, it is certain that evaluations of the potential operational and economic performance of embryonic wave energy technology have been the subject of important distortions.

For example, it is not surprising that wave energy systems appear inflexible when the whole thrust of 1970s/1980s UK policy centred on a notional station of 2 GW capacity, with all the attendant complexities that this brings. Prototype stations with capacities of less than 1 MW might have told a different story, as might the employment of 'tank' tests or experiments. Both the latter options appear now to afford opportunities for trial-and-error learning at relatively low cost, thus pointing the way for future considerations as to the direction of R,D&D. In addition, the large unit size of the South Uist reference station (2 GW) has much to do with the psychological orientation of decision-makers who were used to dealing with very large unit sizes. Furthermore, pessimistic views about the potential of wave energy stemmed in large measure from a bias towards nuclear energy and the poverty of accounting for the relative environmental costs and benefits of renewables. In consideration of the centralization of decision-making processes that this chapter has identified these are influential factors, which for long periods have distorted R,D&D of wave energy technologies and frustrated a more experimental, less discontinuous, approach to technology development in the sector.

Interpreting the wave power case study has broader implications for the themes of this book. Consider, first, the proposition that inflexible decisions will be painful or costly to execute. Clearly, here it is necessary to address contextual issues connected to UK energy policy in the 1970s and 1980s, in order make better sense of the recent history of R,D&D in the area. Thus considered in isolation the cessation of funding for wave power R,D&D in 1982 looks quite good from the point of view of avoiding lumpy investments in infrastructure (content of decisions). The cessation of funding thus may be interpreted as the sensible avoidance of premature commitment to costly research and development, in favour of less risky, gradual learning based on modest operational prototypes (coast of Islay and the Osprey wave stations). On the other hand, consideration of the politics of nuclear power tells a different story, to do with centralized processes of policy-making. In this connection would be cited the determined support of the ETSU and other central actors for continued investment in inflexible nuclear power plant to the detriment of other non-fossil fuel energy supply options, including wave power. Conceived of in this way the viewer sees the costs and distortions of centralized policy-making emphasized in the incremental approach.

Secondly, and relatedly, analyzing a technology development in a 'snapshot' manner foreshortens one's perspective of proceedings. The more recent developments in governmental policy suggest the value of a longitudinal view. A more insightful view of the process by which technology development becomes more or less 'irreversibilized' may thus be promoted. In the case of UK wave power this would mean analysis of the shut-down of central funding as above. However, can conceive of a more fulsome account of progressive learning about wave power technology. This would operate in conjunction with an account of changing governmental approaches to the environment, public-private financing, market stimulation and 'embedded' technology, to illustrate the potential for 'reversibilizing' different supply options in the renewables sector, including wave power. Practically, a key aspect of policy relates to stability. The prospects for ongoing and quicker learning about wave power do not seem to have been well served by the discontinuities in the perception of the potential of wave power and central funding of R,D&D in the area. This is indicative of the delicate balance to be struck between excessive optimism and overdue pessimism about the prospects of new technology, between letting embryonic technology 'stand on its own two feet' in the market place, providing a measure of protection from the vicissitudes of the market and state intervention to help stimulate or open up the market for new sources of, in this case, energy supply. The next Part of the book addresses these aspects of the flexible development of pioneering technology as it reconsiders the findings from the case studies presented herein in terms of the implications for the propositions stated above.

## References

Department of Energy (1985), *Wave Energy - The Department of Energy R&D Programme 1974-1983*, ETSU, Harwell.

DTI (1999a), 'New and Renewable Energy: Prospects for the 21st Century', www.dti.gov.uk/renew/condoc.

DTI (1999b), 'A Fair Deal for Consumer: Modernising the Framework for Utility Regulation – Regulatory, Environmental and Equal Treatment Appraisals', www.dti.gov.uk/urt.

Elliott, D.(1992), 'Renewables and the Privatisation of the UK ESI', *Energy Policy*, vol. 20, pp. 257-68.

Falnes, J. and Lovseth, J. (1991), 'Ocean Wave Energy', *Energy Policy*, vol. 19, pp. 768-775.

Flood, M., Conroy, C. and Gordon, D. (1982), *Eclipse of the Sun? The Future of Renewable Energy Research in Britain*, Friends of the Earth, London.

Flood, M. (1991) *Energy Without End*, Friends of the Earth, London.

Grubb, M. (1990), 'The Cinderella Options a Study of Modernized Renewable Energy Technologies: Part 2 Political and Policy Analysis', *Energy Policy*, vol. 18, pp. 711-25.

Grubb, M. (1991), 'The Integration of Renewable Electricity Sources', *Energy Policy*, vol. 18, pp. 670-688.

Hagerman, G.M. and Heller, T. (1988), 'Wave Energy: a Survey of Twelve Near-term Technologies', *Proceedings of the International Renewable Energy Conference*, Honolulu, HI, 18-24 September, pp. 98-110.

Hamlett, P. (1991), *The Political Construction of Technology*, Personal memorandum, December.

House of Commons Energy Committee (1984), *Ninth Report from the Energy Committee Session 1983-84, Energy Research, Development and Demonstration in the United Kingdom*, HMSO, London.

House of Commons Energy Committee (1992), *Renewable Energy*, HMSO, London.

Hughes, T. (1983), *Networks of Power: Electrification in Western Society: 1880-1930*, John Hopkins University Press, Baltimore, Maryland.

Hughes, T. (1987), 'The Evolution of Large-scale Technological Systems', in W.E. Bijker, T.P. Hughes, and T.J. Pinch, (eds.), *The Social Construction of Technological Systems: New Directions in the Sociology and History of Technology*, MIT Press, Cambridge, Mass., pp. 51-82.

IEA (1991), *Energy Policies of IEA Countries, 1990 Review*, OECD, Paris.

Jeffrey, J. (1990) 'Dirty Tricks: How the Nuclear Lobby Stopped the Development of Wave Power in Britain', *The Ecologist*, vol. 20, pp. 85-90.

Lewis, T. (1985), *Wave Energy*, Graham and Trotman, London.

National Engineering Laboratory (1976), *The Development of Wave Power - A Techno-economic Study*, NEL, Glasgow.

Salter, S. (1988),'World Progress in Wave Energy 1988', *International Journal Of Ambient Energy*, vol. 10, pp. 3-24.

Smith, W. (1991), 'Counting the Cost', *Newsletter of the Network for Alternative Technology and Technology Assessment*, vol. 72, pp. 18-19.

# PART III
# RETROSPECT AND PROSPECT

# 5 Revisiting Incrementalism

## Introduction

The foregoing chapters have demonstrated the dilemma posed by the need to ensure that high profile investments in technology provide the benefits that are often claimed of them by their promoters whilst avoiding the undue costs or harmful consequences often associated with large-scale development or construction projects. In the UK, cases such as the Channel Tunnel, nuclear waste processing, defence technology, the Millennium Dome and Millennium Bridge testify to the currency and relevance of the issues identified in this book. This chapter revisits the case study material presented above with regard to the relevance of incremental approaches to the management and social control of technology. The starting point, and indeed the key theme of this final Part of the book, concerns the validity of analyses and prescriptions flowing from the application of the notion of incrementalism to decision-making involving large-scale technology projects. More specifically, this chapter discusses social control and management of technology as it is addressed by proponents and critics of incrementalism working in the fields of public administration and technology policy, who share a concern for understanding and improving the quality of decision-making in complex or uncertain situations.

In terms of the layout of the chapter, the following section briefly reiterates the notion of incrementalism, which has been applied to the management of large-scale technology projects during the course of this book. Subsequent sections then consider what has been learned from an incremental perspective about technical choice, the evaluation of success and failure of alternative options, and decision processes from the application of such notions to the studies featured above. Finally, the concluding section summarizes the main work and findings of the chapter, in terms of the three propositions underpinning the conduct of the case studies. The following, and concluding, chapter then broadens the horizons of the work in seeking to make connections with the wider literature on the management of innovation and the construction of socially durable technology, and in pointing to some future avenues of research.

**Incrementalism Revisited**

At this juncture it is worth briefly restating the incrementalist ideas that have been central to the arguments presented within this volume. Much is owed to the work of Charles Lindblom, the political scientist who developed the incrementalist approach to managing difficult decision- and policy-making situations, and to David Collingridge who extended and applied this thinking to the realm of technology policy. A point of comparison exists relating to incremental and non-incremental treatments of the control of major technological projects. Some dimensions of this concern the scale and flexibility of decision-making, the appropriateness of alternative structures and processes of decision-making, and the nature and role of analysis and expertise. All of these may be considered in terms of their relevance to the performance (and indeed on what is to count as relevant performance criteria) of large-scale technology projects. An overview of Lindblom's ideas on incrementalism, and their application to the social management of technology, now reopens the discussion.

The work of Charles Lindblom is central to understanding the notion of incrementalism. Several key contributions have helped to define and refine the concept (Lindblom, 1959; 1963; with Braybrooke, 1968; 1977; 1979; 1980; 1990; with Woodhouse, 1993; cf. Quinn, 1980). Lindblom's primary and initial concern was to counter the idea of comprehensive rationality in decision-making, working from an interest in public administration. Unlike the message conveyed in neo-classical economics, 'hard' systems theory, or the statistics-driven RAND approach to operational research, decision-makers are argued to act in a much more 'boundedly rational' and politically aware manner. In particular, incremental decision-making is argued to be (simultaneously) a better description of the practice of decision-making in uncertain circumstances than is provided by the above and also a better prescription for success for decision-makers to follow.

Simply put, demands on information and analysis ensure that for all but the most routine tasks it is extremely difficult to operationalize the kind of linear means-end relationship suggested by the classical notion of rational decision-making, whereby decision-makers seek means to maximize pre-determined objectives (utilities). Decision-making in Lindblom's view is a less heroic, more modest, collective and on-going activity than this. Firstly, means and ends are intertwined and continually adjusted to one another in a process of trial and error. This process is enabled by the consideration of only a limited number of decision options, rather than the whole array of alternatives as dictated by the comprehensive approach. Moreover, the adoption of a decision option is confined to the incremental. In other words, and this is a key aspect of Lindblom's view, small-scale decisions which do not vary much from the status quo are preferred by real-world decision-makers and incrementalism is preferable as a decision-rule for others to follow. Such decisions are deemed to permit greater flexibility or reversibility since the commitments required to support them are less than for more grandiose schemes.

Another critical element of the incremental approach is the observation that small-scale decisions are promoted by decentralized processes. In a genuinely pluralistic political system the influence of dispersed participants may be felt so that the whims of the otherwise powerful few are checked and the policy agenda is shaped by diverse interests. In addition, the dispersal of power among such groups has implications for the analysis of policy; each partisan group will gather data and perform analysis relevant to its particular perspective on a policy matter, thus reducing the burden, or even the need, for any supra-ordinate planning body. In this way a wider range of values may find their way into the processes by which policy is shaped than would otherwise be the case. However, such fragmented analysis may be undermined if social 'probing' is impaired (Lindblom, 1990: Chapter 5), probing being related to the interrogation of alternative processes and options by a variety of constituents. Impaired probing may occur when responsibility for, or influence over, decision-making is concentrated in the hands of a few central actors rather than dispersed, or when the scope of values represented in policy is narrow. The clues to impairment include the inability or unwillingness of citizens to think critically about an issue. Further, the role of large business corporations, overdue reliance on professional technical experts and technology 'pushed' with funding or compliance of governmental bureaucracies all potentially distort decision processes away from the incremental ideal.

For incrementalists, it is thus necessary to understand decision-making processes and impairments thereto in terms of 'the characteristics of the participants, what parts or roles they play, what authority and other powers they hold and how they deal with and control each other' (Lindblom, 1980: 2). The main implication of impaired probing is that certain actors are not as able to contribute effectively to this process of fragmented analysis as they might be. Taken as a whole, incrementalism attends to issues of objective-setting (and the continual redefinition of ends in the light of available means), the scale of decisions, the process and analysis of decision-making and the effectiveness of alternative approaches to making difficult decisions. And underlying all of this is an appreciation of human fallibility and a philosophy which values the avoidance of ills and costs more than the pursuit of ambitious plans which may entail great benefits but also severe risks should they fail (or succeed in the interests of very few).

The case studies discussed above examined the following propositions:

1. decisions to develop inflexible technology projects (i.e. those characterized by high capital intensity, long lead times, large unit size and dependence upon specialized infrastructure) incur unusually painful costs, technically, environmentally, socially or economically;
2. decisions to develop inflexible technology occur as a result of centralized decision-making processes, where the dominance of large organizations able to shed risk onto central government marginalizes legitimate stakeholders (this is where a lack of democratic social control over technological choice is most clearly marked);
3. there are more incremental and flexible alternatives to the selected inflexible technology, some of which may be developed in a relatively decentralized way (this points to the potential operation of more democratic social control over technology).

In addition to those cases providing the empirical material for the chapters above, a number of other case studies have been conducted, which examine the validity of the incremental approach and which have been undertaken by colleagues of the author. The central findings from these various studies are summarized in Tables 5.1, 5.2, 5.3 and 5.4, and refer to work investigating the management of large-scale technology carried out by various combinations of the research team of Collingridge, Genus and James. In terms of the three propositions outlined above a number of findings are common to the case studies that lend support to the incremental thesis.

## Inflexible Technology Projects, Poor Performance

The case studies are all characterized by the construction of technologies involving extraordinarily high costs damaging to the economics of the projects. However, one exception to these findings concerns the apparent breach of incrementalism posed by first generation UK North Sea oil exploration and development. This alone of the cases seems to contradict the thesis that decisions to invest in non-incremental technology projects bearing the hallmarks of inflexibility will incur unduly high costs of development and perform poorly at least in terms of the economics of the project. Whereas some technologies may be considered as representing great technical achievements but at equally great, if not greater social or economic costs, North Sea oil seems to pass both technical and economic hurdles (though one notes the debate about the environmental costs of decommissioning associated with the project). The contribution to the UK Treasury of North Sea oil revenues plus the undoubted technical pioneering that facilitated North Sea field development could be argued to severely dent the validity of incremental prescriptions. Aside from the obvious point that this represents only one case, another argument may be deployed to deny this position. This stems from the falsification of the success of North Sea oil (see Tables 2.3. and 2.4 for a comparison of oilfield economics under different oil price scenarios).

The study of North Sea oil focused upon the development and performance of the early, and most of the largest, North Sea oil fields in the British sector, covering those that commenced production by the end of 1979. The UK treasury has benefited greatly from taxes and royalties from the sector and in 1984 the UK became a net exporter of crude oil. However, the falsification of the success of North Sea oil turns on the view that decision- makers may take no comfort in serendipitously 'getting it right'. In other words, but for the fortuitous and unforeseen high level of oil prices present at the time many of the relevant oil fields came on stream, the economic performance of the investment decisions involved would have been much worse. Moreover, the inflexibility of the technology chosen to exploit fields such as Forties, Brent and Piper (for example the extremely large platforms) meant that decision-makers simply had to have faith in decisions once they were made; these could not be reversed cheaply. Put simply, extrapolations were made by executives, in Shell and Exxon, for example, based on prevailing trends in oil prices prior to the OPEC crisis of 1973/4 and existing around the time that vital investment development decisions were being taken (County NatWest Woodmac, 1989; Odell and Rosing, 1980; Reid, 1987). These scenarios built in more modest but still quite generous allowances of 2% growth per annum in oil prices over the lifetime of the fields concerned (Table 2.3). Unfortunately, the result of this applying this scenario makes for gloomy reading, for the economics of the various fields (as measured in terms of discounted cash flow with a benign discount rate of 15% per annum) is markedly and adversely affected. Hence the falsification of the success of North Sea oil decision-making enables incrementalism to be retained.

Turning to other case study examples, it may be noted that the Channel Tunnel has been a similarly difficult project in terms of the burgeoning costs of its construction, which have risen by roughly 70% over the 1986 estimates, and in terms of financing costs that have nearly doubled over the same period (see Table 3.3). Capital expenditure on the Space Shuttle was less than $1 billion dollars in 1961 but over $6 billion in 1966 (1967 US dollars) (Collingridge and James, 1990) and nuclear power has been notoriously costly to develop both economically and environmentally. Amongst projects of the type discussed here estimates of capital intensities of 75% are not untypical (see Table 5.2). Thus where, the capital intensity of the Channel Tunnel has been estimated at 82%, 80% is typical for early UK North Sea oil fields, whilst for nuclear plant an (optimistic) figure closer to 50% was quoted early in the construction of French PWR plant, which were regarded as more successful than their US and UK counterparts (Collingridge, 1992). A great deal of caution needs to be exercised in the interpretation of the wave power case study, here. First of all the case concentrates on the UK experience with wave power in the 1970s and 1980s, when governmental confidence in and support for wave energy began to decline. As discussed previously (Chapter 4) one of the key factors in the demise of wave power concerned the large-scale mind-set of influential actors who provided estimates of reliability and unit costs, or who determined the size of demonstration prototypes. Remarks about the inflexibility of embryonic wave energy technology and performance need therefore to be read with this note of caution in mind.

Relatedly, two further points may be made regarding the implications of inflexible technology projects for the cost and control of errors in decision-making. First, the discovery of the extent of the capital intensity of large-scale technology projects occurs some way into the life of an investment. This is related to the lead time of the project concerned which may be understood as the period during which data becomes available on the costs or benefits of the technology. The lead time for development for the large scale projects discussed above was of the order of 6-8 years (though the figure is indicative for UK wave power, for which there is little operational experience on which to base a more definitive analysis). In addition, the point at which it may safely be said that a project has been of net benefit (or otherwise) can be extraordinarily long - 30 to 40 years in the case of nuclear plant having an operational life of about 25 years. What this means for decision-making is that for ongoing programmes involving concurrent investments is that learning about the accuracy of forecasted capital costs is slow. This connects to the second point about unit size since if the total capacity of the project is made up of a few giant units (platforms in an oil field, a tunnel under a sea, wave energy or nuclear power plant, and so on) there is less opportunity to learn about the behaviour of costs. Moreover, when that learning does occur there may be little opportunity to apply it to subsequent units. In short, inflexible technology projects, characterized by high capital intensity, long lead times, large unit size, and also by dependence upon specialized infrastructure exacerbates the likelihood, discovery, costs and remediation of errors of decision-making.

**Table 5.1 Case studies of large-scale technology projects: summary**

| | Inflexible Technology Project | Performance | Centralized decision-making |
|---|---|---|---|
| North Sea oil (UK) | yes | good | yes |
| Channel Tunnel (UK) | yes | poor | yes |
| Wave energy (UK)* | yes | poor | yes |
| Large irrigation schemes (developing countries) | yes | poor | yes |
| Nuclear power: France | yes | poor | yes |
| UK | yes | poor | yes |
| US | yes | poor | yes |
| Space shuttle | yes | poor | yes |
| System-built high-rise buildings (UK) | yes | poor | yes |
| Videotex (France) | yes | poor | yes |

* Wave energy estimates based on ETSU assumptions.

*Sources*: Author; Collingridge (1990; 1992); Collingridge, Genus and James (1994).

## Inflexible Technology, Centralized Decision-making

Moving on to the second proposition stated above, the question is posed as to whether decisions to construct inflexible technology are associated, typically, with centralized processes for decision-making. The short answer to this question is 'yes'. The extent of centralization may be understood with reference to a number of factors. In the programme of case studies referred to in this chapter the issue has been analyzed by identifying the protagonists central to decision-making then, in contrast, focusing upon the marginalization of 'missing actors' from the decision-making process (see Table 5.3). All of this is bound up with the matter of the extent and timing of debate (probing) concerning crucial investment and technical decisions, particularly that pertaining to potential alternative technical solutions or organizational arrangements.

**Table 5.2 Capital intensity in large-scale technology projects**

(Capital expenditure expressed as a percentage of total lifetime project costs)

| | |
|---|---|
| North Sea oil (UK) (range for early fields) | 50-85 |
| Channel Tunnel (UK) (1994 estimate) | 80 |
| Wave energy | 60-95 |
| Large irrigation schemes (developing countries) | n/a[a] |
| Nuclear power: | |
| France | 50 |
| United Kingdom | 60-70 |
| United States | 60-70 |
| Space shuttle | 95 |
| System-built high-rise buildings (UK) | 60 |
| Videotex (France) | n/a[b] |

*Notes:* a. The costs of development for irrigation schemes in developing schemes have been estimated at about $15 billion per annum, with an average cost overrun of roughly 40%.

b. 1980s expenditure on Videotex reached $400 million p.a. in Britain, France and Germany.

*Sources*: Author; Collingridge (1990; 1992); Collingridge, Genus and James (1994); Hagerman and Heller (1988).

The central actors in the case studies may be cited as follows: the role of construction companies is key to the specification of the contract governing the construction of Channel Tunnel infrastructure (along with the funding banks) and in the construction of system built housing in the UK (along with the Ministry of Housing). In the case of North Sea oil the major oil companies were the central players in conjunction with the Department of Energy, offices of which also played a defining role in the evaluation of the prospects for wave power technology. In both the recent history of UK renewable energy sources and in the story of nuclear power in that country, the UK Atomic Energy Authority has played a critical role in the direction and level of support given to various energy options. The US and French equivalents of UKAEA together with the electricity generators in those countries were similarly important to continued support for nuclear power. NASA is cited as the main player in the development of the Space Shuttle, whilst the World Bank has been central to

**Table 5.3 'Missing actors' from decision-making about large-scale technology projects**

| | |
|---|---|
| North Sea oil (UK) | 'Dissenting' energy analysts, independent oil companies |
| Channel Tunnel (UK) | The 'owner' - Eurotunnel, incorporated after 'polo mint' contract |
| Wave power | Developers |
| Large irrigation schemes (developing countries) | Farmers |
| Nuclear power (France, UK and USA) | Investors and insurers |
| Space shuttle | Scientists and satellite launchers |
| System-built high-rise flats (UK) | Tenants |
| Videotex (France) | Users |

*Sources*: Author; Collingridge (1990; 1992); Collingridge, Genus and James (1994).

the promotion of large irrigation schemes in developing countries. Finally, in a variety of countries the development of videotex (viewdata information technology) was dominated by (then) state-owned post, telegraph and telecommunications organizations (Collingridge, 1992). By contrast, actors who have been marginalized from the process of technology development include: independent oil companies and energy analysts (North Sea oil); Eurotunnel (operator of the services which run through the Channel tunnel); developers of energy devices (wave power); scientists and satellite launchers (Space Shuttle), investors, insurers and public utility bodies (nuclear power) and users (farmers, tenants and customers) of irrigation equipment, high-rise flats and videotex viewdata systems.

The familiar tale is one of large corporations and governmental bodies able to promote big projects according to utopian visions and plans, devised remotely from those who will be most affected by their implementation. If this alone was not cause enough for concern, one must also mention the tendency for the financial risks associated with such high profile large-scale technology decisions to be shifted onto the public purse. The Channel Tunnel case is especially interesting in this respect being usually regarded as being a private project, where central government has been able to avoid taking on the financial risks of the project and, moreover, has been able to get private sector organizations to accept them. Closer scrutiny, however, shows that both the British and French governments played a significant role in ensuring that the necessary legislation was passed to enable a rapid move to start construction following the signing of the Treaty of Canterbury in 1986. Further, the Thatcher and Mitterand governments also gave important (though informal) guarantees to ensure the necessary financing of the project. Meanwhile, those who often get to pay for grandiose schemes (at least indirectly through their taxes and state expenditure), often find it difficult to get their voices heard in this process of decision-making. Similarly, those with dissenting views about the political economy of an investment or the feasibility of a proposed technical design are also often unable to influence the direction of policy.

## More Flexible Alternatives?

Having identified very briefly the central players (and non-players) in each of the cases what implications are there for probing and decision-making? The extent to which the probing of policy is proscribed or foreshortened in cases such as those referred to above is well testified. For example, it is clear that the view that Eurotunnel as operator of Channel Tunnel services took of the tunnel's design was at odds with that of the contractor, TransManche Link. However, in the build-up of momentum that seems to accompany, if not be necessitated by, the promotion of large-scale commitments, Eurotunnel was not able to express a view about its preferred design. One reason for this was simply because it did not exist at the time that crucial decisions about design were being taken. A second factor was that Eurotunnel was short of staff and expertise for some time after its incorporation when many critical activities were being undertaken, and was thus less able to scrutinize the contractor's work or to rewrite specifications than it was later in the play. Not that Eurotunnel would necessarily have advocated a less sophisticated design had its voice been heard during 1985-6 when the construction contract governing the design specifications was being drawn up between the banks and the constructors. Rather, at the risk of excessive repetition, the basic point being made flows from the recognition that a key stakeholder in the Channel Tunnel case was a missing actor. The implications of this for technical choice is that when the firm did enter the fray there was fierce disagreement with the contractor about the technical specifications that should have formed the basis of contracts governing various elements of the design and construction of Channel Tunnel. Indeed, this disagreement extended to the process of contracting, connected to how the work carried out and the contracts relating thereto, should have been dispersed among a number of contractors each having expertise in the specific different elements of the project.

Other cases also make the point that potentially more incremental and flexible decision options are denied an airing due to the centralized and circumscribed nature of decision-making. In the case of North Sea oil one can point to the nature of the regime for awarding licences to blocks of the North Sea to be explored for oil. Here, the 'unholy communion' between the major oil companies and officials at the Department of Energy during the 1960s and 1970s has been cited. This has worked against the participation of the 'independent' oil firms which, not having pockets as deep as the 'majors', tended to favour more flexible technical designs in fields for which they did win licences. An example of this is the Argyll field where Hamilton Oil employed a converted drilling rig as a floating production platform.

In the nuclear power cases the absence of investors may be cited, for example in the UK the eventual decentralization of electricity generation saw a resounding rejection of nuclear energy as an attractive investment by the City. Would-be investors were quite wary of the actual and potential future costs involved in operation, storage and decommissioning. (Part of the new assessment sprung from the application of higher discount rates by the private sector compared to the public sector). In addition, despite the protracted public inquiries into Windscale and Sizewell B plants, for instance, critical reports by a plethora of pressure groups and governmental bodies failed to influence decisions. Secrecy became endemic regarding the work and cost calculations about nuclear power undertaken by the Atomic Energy Authority and the Central Electricity Generating Board. The freeing up of criticism on the subject, as illustrated by the campaign against nuclear power by the National Coal Board from the mid-1960s, came only after irreversible decisions to proceed with the programme had been taken (irreversible that is with regard to the sunk costs involved, not irreversible in any absolute sense). A similar story applies to US experience with nuclear power except that in America the nuclear project was abandoned in the mid-1970s, fifteen years before Britain. Essentially, the situation in the post-war years saw central government taking on the risks of insuring and restricting the liability to owners of plant of potential nuclear accidents under conditions of high economic growth and rising energy demand. The late-1960s onward saw a period of rising inflation, interest rates, and uncertain demand and with it the realization that smaller schemes involving less capital investment, and the pursuit of a diversity of supply sources including renewable energy, might be a more appropriate strategy for the energy utilities to follow (Collingridge, 1992).

There is, then, a third key finding from the case studies. This is that, in addition to inflexible decisions regarding large-scale technology incurring undue costs and being associated with centralized decision-making processes, more flexible alternatives exist which could have been implemented in a more decentralized manner. This is so for most of the case studies referred to above (see Table 5.4).

**Table 5.4 Flexible alternatives to large-scale technology projects**

| | |
|---|---|
| North Sea oil | Converted drilling rigs, licensing of fields by auction rather than central choice |
| Channel Tunnel | Dispersed investment in ferries, rail, air, award contracts by expertise |
| Wave power (UK) | Small, low capacity reference stations, tank testing for prototypes |
| System-built high-rise buildings (UK) | Low-rise accommodation, housing cooperatives |
| Large irrigation schemes | Tube wells financed privately |
| Nuclear power (France, UK, USA) | Conventional generating plant, some renewable sources |
| Space shuttle | Russian approach to space technology |
| Videotex (France) | Diverse viewdata systems privately financed |

It has already been mentioned that for nuclear power a number of alternative energy sources fundable by private investors and bearing less risk for stakeholders were available. Two other examples (the Channel Tunnel and the space shuttle) will suffice to illustrate further the current point. Thus it may be argued that the opportunity cost of investing in Channel Tunnel technology is the resources which could have been allocated to improving various aspects of cross-Channel air, sea and rail transport. In addition, even the construction of the tunnel could have proceeded in a more decentralized manner. For example, it is now widely recognised that a mistake was made in granting the construction contract for various aspects of the work to a sole contractor (or rather consortium) that had very little expertise in certain aspects of the work. (The consortium that comprised the contractor was made up of building firms, which were used to civil engineering rather than transport engineering projects.) It would have been more appropriate to award contracts for the relevant tunnelling, fixed equipment, and rolling stock purchasing elements of the project according to the experience of the bidder, as there was in any case a Maitre d'Oeuvre in place to oversee the coordination of the project as a whole. The interview material and literature about the project reveal that the decision to centralize the award and conduct of the contract work was more to do with preserving the self-interest of various building companies and banks, than it was to do with conducting the project work in the most cost-efficient and effective manner.

In the case of the space shuttle, the approach taken by the USSR/Russian Federation with regard to space exploration demonstrates a more flexible approach than NASA's (despite recent difficulties with the Mir space station). Technically, the emphasis has been on the use of expendable rockets and incremental developments of long-established designs, whereas NASA has tended to abandon existing technologies in favour of 'the next gigantic leap to some new promised land where all the technical troubles will be solved. Its projects have been consistently too big' (Collingridge, 1990: 192). Whilst Soviet/Russian technology has been less ambitious technically and costlier to operate than its US counterpart, capital costs have been lower and the upgrading of satellite technology less lumpy thus reducing the potential cost of error. There has been a diversity of equipment used for satellite launching, compared to the American experience where the costs of developing the Space Shuttle has necessitated its more intensive use to recoup sunk costs. Reliance upon one item in this way places a project in a situation of great vulnerability since sensitivity to changes affecting the schedule and costs of the project is pronounced.

Whilst details of the organization of Soviet space exploration remain sketchy, it is not difficult to construct an alternative decentralized model for managing space technology. This puts diversity centre-stage, allowing satellite launchers a range of providers and systems from which to select. For the US the implications of this began to be recognized with consideration by the National Space Council of the need for other organizations to play a leading role in trips to the Moon or Mars (Collingridge, 1990). Similarly, the role of space scientists could be strengthened. (They had complained that NASA was ignoring their views, for example over the development of the Earth Observing System.) Here, the end users' influence could be enhanced by allowing them to buy space on launchers or space stations thus generating competition as the scientists choose between potential investments in different technologies. The next section draws together the main findings and contribution of these studies.

## Conclusion

This chapter has retreated from the detail of the case studies featured in Part II of the book. Instead, more general arguments have been considered concerning the implications for incrementalist approaches to decision-making of the research reported in this book. The basic orientation of the research discussed above has been to focus upon examining propositions associated with incrementalism employing cases of large-scale decision-making. In other words, the latter constitute non-incremental decisions that, by definition, were not taken in accordance with the principles of incrementalism. The search has been for indications that decisions such as these, which breach the incremental prescription, have been successful at least in financial terms if not with regard to other values. The discovery of such a class of decisions would pose a severe challenge to incrementalism. More broadly, the research has aimed to explain non-incremental decision-making (c.f. Lustick, 1980; Rajagopalan and Rasheed, 1995; Schulman, 1975). In doing so, the case studies juxtapose the difficulties encountered in the implementation of large-scale technology projects with the potential benefits of more flexible alternative decision options and processes. There are therefore a number of ways in which the material contained in this book contributes to the extant literature. These are summarized below.

Firstly, as referred to in the previous paragraph, there are clear implications for decision-makers of contravening the prescriptions of incrementalism set out at various points in this volume. Though there is some need for care in interpreting the recent history of wave power in the UK, the case studies presented above breach the stated rules concerning the adoption of flexible decisions and serve to demonstrate the potential errors and costs that are incurred in so doing. In continuing the extension of the notion of incrementalism from its original base in decision theory/public administration to understanding the management of large-scale technology, these studies augment an accumulating body of knowledge that points up the significance of flexible decision-making (they are not merely one-off cases). In relation to the question of the scale of decisions, the studies demonstrate and provide measures for inflexibility. The data by which inflexibility may be analyzed are not discovered *ex ante*, such discovery occurs with the process of development and is subject to negotiation or interpretation (as the next chapter will further consider). Nevertheless, one of the strengths of the incremental approach is that there is little requirement to acquire the precise data in advance, as demanded by the synoptic approach to decision-making. The main point is that decision-makers should be aware of the broad significance of factors such as capital intensity and dependence upon specialized infrastructure, and seek to favour commitments that more easily facilitate the detection and correction of error. Essentially, the cost of indivisible commitments is non-incremental investment which may yield great benefit but which also make for expensive trial and error. Incrementalism, meanwhile, prizes early and low-cost trial and error, which in technology management and policy terms requires the adoption of public policies or corporate strategies favouring flexible, modular technology.

A related second point concerns the connection between the content of technology decisions (whether flexible or inflexible) and decision processes. Jones' (1975) study of speculative augmentation (in his public satisfying model) emphasizes the role of public opinion in promoting non-incremental policies. Contrary to Jones' view, this study highlights the manner in which pioneering or glamorous adventures in technology development may be 'pushed', either in an atmosphere of cosy consent about the goodness of a project or to the neglect of potentially affected parties. To the extent that this occurs the nature and implications of nondecision-making (Bachrach and Baratz, 1962) are reinforced. The values that come to be most influential in particular cases are those pertaining to groups that, deliberately or not, mobilize support for certain technical and administrative options, or for certain processes by which the related decision-making occurs. This seems to lend some credence to Rajagopalan and Rasheed's, (1995) proposition regarding the role of leadership vision and a sense of mission in driving non-incremental decisions. Whilst they stress the role of individual chief executives within the firm in leading transformational change, the cases presented above testify to the part played by coalitions in various private and public organizations in articulating the need for major initiatives (or not, in the case of wave power). Making criticism work to challenge conventional wisdom seems to be difficult in such an atmosphere of heightened purpose, as the North Sea, Channel Tunnel and wave power cases all demonstrate in their various ways. The nature and remedy of impairments to probing of technology is central to the debate and selection of socially responsive (and responsible) decisions in the area, as discussed in the next chapter.

Thirdly, this book makes a contribution to the literature with respect to some issues of method. Thirty years ago, Theodore Lowi (1970) criticized 'The Policy-making Process' (Lindblom, 1968) for what he saw as its ill-attention to the specific content and context of decision-making, and for failing to distinguish between decision-making, policy-making and policy-making in firms (strategy, in other words). The basic danger referred to by Lowi has been recognized and dealt with here. The substantive content of policy-making (in this book distinguished as 'public' technology policy and 'private' corporate strategy) does need to be analyzed if we wish to improve our appreciation of rival models of decision-making, which incrementalism included, tend to have been advanced in an abstract and general form. The approach taken here, addressing the historical development of large-scale technology, has been to create a picture, no doubt incomplete, of macro- and organizational-level contexts and actions and of the interrelationships between these. As these have emerged, and as operational experience has been gained, it has been possible to interpret results against the backdrop of the theoretical framework of incremental decision-making established above, and thus to make some inferences regarding the prescriptive validity of incrementalism. Thus some insight has been gained into the merits of rival decision-making approaches on the basis of rich descriptions of specific cases; even if this does make generalization across different cases hazardous, some intelligent observations can be, and have been, tested and made.

The research strategy taken here is by no means the only possible approach to investigating the issues under scrutiny. For example another method would be to analyze incremental decisions that prove to be very costly (cf. research on corporate strategy by Johnson (1987) and Miller (1992)). Such an approach could be very revealing and damaging to the incremental position, as implied by the view concerning threshold or 'sleeper' effects of incremental decisions which at a certain point can lead to disastrous consequences (e.g. incremental pollution of the environment). Against this, though, it may be objected that an alternative approach to dealing with complexity or uncertainty would still have to be shown to perform better than incrementalism. However we await, still, studies of practice that might lend credence to such a proposition. Equally, the explanation of sleeper effects (analyzing the chaotic threshold effects of incremental decisions), which has not been to the fore in this particular study, remains an area as short of empirical investigation now as when Rajagopalan and Rasheed (1995) identified it as a potentially fruitful area of inquiry.

Finally, as with any research, there are some limitations of this study that need to be acknowledged. It is proposed that attending to these is best achieved in conjunction with an identification of the standing of the work within a wider body of relevant literature than has been the case in this particular chapter. To this end the following, and final, chapter connects the research reported here to broader concerns regarding the management of innovation, and the socially constructed and indeterminate nature of technology.

## References

Bachrach, P. and Baratz, M.S. (1962), 'Two Faces of Power', *American Political Science Review*, vol. 56, pp. 947-952.

Braybrooke, D. and Lindblom, C.E. (1963), *A Strategy of Decision: Policy Evaluation as a Social Process*, Free Press, New York.

Collingridge, D. (1982), *Critical Decision Making: a New Theory of Social Choice*, Frances

Pinter, London.
Collingridge, D. (1989, 11 November), *Personal correspondence.*
Collingridge, D. (1990), 'Technology, Organizations and Incrementalism; the Space Shuttle', *Technology Analysis and Strategic Management*, vol. 2, pp. 181-200.
Collingridge, D. (1992), *The Management of Scale*, Routledge, London.
Collingridge, D., Genus, A. and James, P. (1994), 'Inflexibility in the Development of North Sea Oil', *Technological Forecasting and Social Change*, vol. 45, pp. 169-188.
County Natwest Woodmac (1989 and various issues), *North Sea service*, National Westminster Bank, Aberdeen.
Douglas, M. and Wildavsky, A. (1982), *Risk and Culture: an Essay on the Selection of Technical and Environmental Dangers*, University of California Press, Los Angeles.
Hagerman, G.M. and Heller, T. (1988), 'Wave Energy: a Survey of Twelve Near-term Technologies', *Proceedings of the International Renewable Energy Conference*, Honolulu, HI, 18-24 September.
Johnson, G. (1987), *Strategic Change and the Management Process*, Blackwell, Oxford.
Jones, C.O. (1975), *Clean Air: the Policies and Politics of Pollution Control*, University of Pittsburgh Press, Pittsburgh.
Lindblom, C.E. (1959), 'The Science of Muddling Through', *Public Administration Review*, vol. 19, pp. 79-88.
Lindblom, C.E. (1968), *The Policy-making Process*, Prentice-Hall, New Jersey.
Lindblom, C.E. (1977), *Politics and Markets*, Basic Books, New York.
Lindblom, C.E. (1979), 'Still muddling not yet through', *Public Administration Review*, vol. 39, pp. 517-527.
Lindblom, C.E. (1980), *The Policy Making Process* (2nd edition), Prentice-Hall, New Jersey.
Lindblom, C.E. (1989, 4 October), *Personal correspondence.*
Lindblom, C.E. (1990), *Inquiry and Change*, Yale University Press, New Haven.
Lindblom, C.E. and Woodhouse, E.J. (1993), *The Policy Making Process* (3rd edition), Prentice-Hall, New Jersey.
Lowi, T. (1970), 'Decision Making vs. Policy Making: Toward an Antidote for Technocracy', *Public Administration Review*, vol. 30, pp. 314-425.
Lustick, I. (1980), 'Explaining the Variable Utility of Disjointed Incrementalism', *American Political Science Review*, vol. 74, pp. 442-453.
Miller, D. (1992), *The Icarus paradox*, Harper Business, New York, NY.
Morone, J.G. and Woodhouse, E.J. (1989), *The Demise of Nuclear Energy? Lessons for Democratic Control of Technology*, Yale University Press, New Haven.
Odell, P. and Rosing, K.E. (1980), *The Future of Oil*, Kogan Page, London.
Quinn, J.B. (1980), *Strategies for Change: Logical Incrementalism*, Irwin, Homewood, IL.
Rajagopalan, N. and Rasheed, A.M.A. (1995), 'Incremental Models of Policy Formulation and Non-incremental Changes: Critical Review and Synthesis', *British Journal of Management*, vol. 6, pp. 289-302.
Reid, R. (1987), 'A View of European Oil and Gas Issues' in J. Rees and P. Odell, *The International Oil Industry*, Macmillan, London. p. 78.
Schulman, P. (1975), 'Non-incremental Policy Making: Notes Toward an Alternative Paradigm', *American Political Science Review*, vol. 74, pp. 342-353.
Winner, L. (1977), *Autonomous Technology: Technics out of Control as a Theme in Political Thought*, MIT, Cambridge, MA.

# 6 Making Connections

## Introduction

This chapter offers further reflections on decision-making and the social management of large-scale technology. In particular, it seeks to connect the material presented in the foregoing chapters of this volume to the wider literature on the somewhat underrepresented topic of failed, or failing, innovation and to recent developments in the construction of technology. In their different ways, and to varying degrees, the case studies presented in Part II illustrate factors contributing to difficulties of project management, problems for the 'social control' of technology (Collingridge, 1980), and for managing risky or uncertain investments in technology. In consideration of the various ways in which decisions and failure have been conceptualized and accounted for the chapter compares determinate and indeterminate perspectives of technology development. At the heart of the chapter is the notion that conventional views of decision-making and technology development may need to be rethought, including some that inform the research reported above. In particular, issues of temporality, interpretation and process need to be better addressed if an improved analysis of decision-making and technology and management is to be obtained.

There is a vast literature and a common perception regarding the benefits of technology and innovation to macro-economic and organizational health. Conventionally, the focus of researchers in the area of technology and innovation management has been to identify key factors for enabling successful innovation or research and development. This research has examined the nature and implications of national systems of innovation, relationships between science policy, technology policy and competitiveness (of firms and nations or regions), or organizational or network structures for innovation. Often in this work developments in technology, or product innovation, are accepted unquestioningly as good for society, or good for the firm. Or, the values by which these benefits might be evaluated are narrow to the extent that a technical or an economic rationality predominates to the neglect of other types of value. In contrast, relatively little has been said to qualify notions of success or benefit, or to tackle directly the nature and sources of the failure and costs of technology development. And yet this is despite acknowledged difficulties associated with major projects (Hall, 1980; Morris and Hough, 1987; Shapira and Berndt, 1997, in addition to the cases presented above) and the high rates of failure associated with innovative, especially radically innovative, product development activities (35-45% of new product development projects result in failure, according to Boulding et al, 1997). Thus this is an area of neglect in need of attention if a better understanding of the intricacies of analyzing and managing technological innovation is to be developed. It is the aim of this chapter to contribute to such development.

In much of the literature, contributions on the success and failure of technological innovation are imbued with a determinate orientation towards the subject under scrutiny. Here, the term determinate denotes any tendency on the part of researchers to treat the design of technology as ultimate and social issues related to the use or implications of the technology as closed (Wynne, 1995; Grint and Woolgar, 1997). Determinateness connects to problems and preferences of concept and method. More determinate analyses of innovation may privilege technology over the social (though social determinism implies the reverse), separate the technical from the social 'elements' of innovation or, temporally-speaking, impose a snapshot view of the completion of design or implementation activities. Further, the analysis of innovation, including the evaluation of success or failure, may be presented in an objectivized or context-insensitve fashion. By referring to determinateness and indeterminateness contributions on the success and failure of technology development may be interrogated from a critical standpoint and some avenues and difficulties for future research on technology policy and management identified.

As in previous chapters, the following sections raise issues connected to the construction, assessment and management of large-scale technology based on a reading of literature from three broad perspectives of technological development and innovation:

1. evolutionary/Schumpeterian/alternative economics (relating to the nature of the selection environment, or the link between innovation and the competitive market position of the firm);
2. technology management/organization theory/project management (typically revealing a concern with innovation strategy, the functional distribution of resources within the firm, the coordination of R&D with other functional activities, and structures for innovation and creativity);

3. sociology of science & technology (including developments in the history of technology; the social shaping of technology; social constructivism; actor network theory; and the ethnography of innovation and technical change).

In addition the work of the chapter is advanced through consideration of the following questions that seem most pertinent to the subject under review. First, what does it mean to speak of the failure of technological innovation and how helpful are determinate versus indeterminate approaches to this question? Secondly, how should we improve our understanding of the economic evaluation of technological innovation and decision-making? Thirdly, what implications are there for conceptualizing decision-making and failure of taking seriously the social aspects of technology development and innovative activities? Similarly, in what ways do more historically- or contextually-sensitive treatments of innovation qualify conventional notions of decision-making and the failure of innovation?

The remainder of this chapter is organized into two further sections as follows. The next section considers what has been learned about the management of large-scale technology in terms of failed decision-making or project organization. In doing so it explores the issues from the perspective of the techno-economic evaluation of innovation. Subsequent to this, the final section of the book addresses social aspects of the construction of large-scale technology, with particular reference to constructive technology assessment, to indicate points of contact between the approach taken here, CTA and the wider body of research on social shaping and construction of technology. This may enable the better identification of factors that seem to promote or are involved in the design or negotiation of what counts as 'good' or failing technology. In each of these sections what is of interest is the possibility that determinate approaches foreshorten our view of the failure of technology development Further, the prospect is raised that our understanding of technology development is skewed by an underlying presumption of certainty and stability or by neglect of some issues of temporality, process and context.

## Decision-making, Technology and 'Failure'

Technological innovation is widely accepted as being the commercialization of a new product or process. The dilemma of radical or large-scale innovation is represented by the possibility of sizeable financial gains to be won by the successful commercialization of a new product or process but also by the commitment of vast resources to R&D and product launch activities against the backdrop of a high risk of loss. In analyzing successful and failed innovation researchers in phase I of Project Sappho distinguished between pairs of innovations in the chemical and scientific instrument sectors in terms of their ability to attract a market and/or to earn a profit (SPRU, 1972). (Regardless of technical capacity these were the criteria on which the innovations were to be evaluated.) More specifically, the standard approach to be found in the literature on managerial decision-making, and employed in the case studies above, proposes a calculation of the discounted cash flows anticipated from an investment. This approach conceives of the failure of innovation as having occurred when the discounted net present value of future cash flows of the investment is negative.

The SPRU researchers' approach to analyzing innovations and innovating firms is of a type wherein the economic criteria by which success or failure is adjudged are applied from without. Such research is determinate to the extent that what is presented is an account of the performance of innovations that seems to close the book on the subject; there is little room for the negotiation or reinterpretation of success/failure or the (economic) criteria chosen as the basis for making the evaluation. The case studies reported in this book have been analyzed, in part, in terms of their estimated lifetime discounted cash flows and internal rates of return. The discussion of performance in studies like these turns upon a characterization of the self-interests of the promoters of such projects (itself a problematic matter) and an understanding, though not specific investigation, of the investment criteria (or hurdle rates) preferred by decision-makers in the sector concerned. In preparing the North Sea oil case study informal discussions with industry analysts (at County NatWest Woodmac) revealed differences in discount rates employed by oil companies, according to their view of the risks involved in exploring different types of oil province. An investment in a pioneering sector like the North Sea could be subject to discount rates of 40% while more familiar exploration efforts on land might attract a discount factor of 15%. Moreover, managers in different companies used different rules of thumb to guide decisions about investment in similar areas of oil exploration. The use of scenarios on the basis of historical, current and future estimated prices and costs (provided in discussions with industry analysts and archive material containing the views of industry managers) enables quite a sensitive picture to be drawn of the changing expectations and investment criteria of key decision-makers.

There are a number of observations to be made regarding reliance upon investment appraisal techniques such as NPV analysis, or the identification of cost or time overruns for the evaluation of major projects. Firstly, these provide rather narrow criteria that miss indirect benefits and so understate returns that accrue far into the future or in ways not easily connected with the particular investment presently under review (Shapira and Berndt, 1997). Secondly, whereas Wildavsky's (1987) notion of the 'paradox of time' invites consideration of the link between past success and future failure, cases such as investment in the europrocessor construe the failure of a major project as representing a step in the learning process that characterizes eventually successful technology development (Molina, 1998; c.f. Schilling, 1988). As Shapira and Berndt observe, the success or failure of 'grand-scale construction projects', such as Brooklyn Bridge or Sydney Opera House, is open to reconstruction (though it was not an aim of their work to define how or in what ways such reconstruction occurs). Third, and more generally, the type of thinking implicit in research on large-scale innovations stops short of what MacKenzie (1992) calls an 'ethnoaccountancy' of technology related to how the evaluation of the financial performance of technological innovations actually occurs compared with the prescriptions of economic theory. Some other theoretical and empirical research identifies national, institutional or organizational cultural aspects of decision-making leading to short-termist horizons with respect to financing R&D, for example (Grinyer et al, 1998; Hayes and Garvin, 1982; Jacobs, 1991). There remains a dearth of evidence concerning the evaluation and management of apparently failing innovation, however, ethnographic or otherwise.

The research reported here was originally inspired by a concern for technology development at the public policy and inter-organizational levels rather more than it was by intra-firm considerations. However, with regard to radical innovation projects within the firm two interesting, possibly contradictory, insights stemming from interview-based or experimental research designs seem to merit mention in terms of prospective future study. First is senior managers' lack of specification of economic criteria on which to evaluate product innovation until after the launch of a project, leaving subordinates charged with the day-to-day development activities to 'shoot at a moving target in which their failure is preordained' (Bart, 1999). There is a resonance here with large-scale projects such as the Channel Tunnel where the contractor and client have argued vehemently and in the courts about the proper definition and interpretation of technical and other specifications of elements of the work (see Chapter 3). Secondly, the continued and escalated commitment of managers to a 'losing course of action' in the area of new product development has been ascribed to 'managers' bias toward optimism and sense of control over risk' (Boulding et al, 1997). Also, Thomas (cited in Freeman, 1982) noted that engineers in two scientific instrument firms tended to conservatively estimate costs of development in order to build into estimates the 'technical feeling' an engineer has about a project). Intriguingly, the study by Boulding and colleagues considered differences in the definition of success and failure of product development projects to be less important to the management of failing innovation efforts, and in particular the stop/don't stop decision, than the question of managers' perception of their own control abilities. Also of consequence is the conclusion that better understanding and management of failure of innovation may be facilitated by the addition of new decision-makers as the innovation project proceeds – the 'decoupling' of the go/no go decision-maker from the stop/no-stop decision-maker (Boulding et al, 1997). Mindful of the tendency to equate decision-making about complex projects with choices exercised by a single individual, these remarks do point up the significance of personal and micro-political aspects of project evaluation.

There is an interesting unit of analysis issue here. As mentioned previously, the motivation behind the case study research undertaken by the author is a concern to identify aspects of public policy, inter-organizational relations and technoscience affecting the course of large-scale technology projects. As such there is relatively little attention to micro-organizational or individual-level factors. There are potentially fruitful avenues to explore in these directions. For example, take the following contrasting views on the issue of lead time. With regard to corporate new product development projects, one holds that a 'fountain model' of concurrent engineering enables inter-project learning and improved coordination between project and other knowledge bases in the firm. Here the setting of very tight deadlines for completion of a project (more specifically Ericsson Japan's cellular telephone system project) enables a 'coupling logic'. The argument is that tight non-negotiable deadlines affect the attention of individuals 'inducing' them to work out for themselves what they need to be able solve problems to accomplish specific goals, seeking an sharing knowledge from others or from past projects (Lindkvist et al, 1998). The implication for managing complex technology projects is that ambitious deadlines can enhance coordination within projects, leading to the abandonment of sequential, 'over-the-wall' approaches to development in favour of parallel working. (This may be contrasted with the caution advised regarding concurrency in the above case studies, particularly with regard to the construction of the Channel Tunnel.) Such an approach, it is claimed, is suitable for projects where error detection is difficult 'due to the systemic context [of development] producing many unforeseeable errors', and thus may contribute to shortening lead times (Lindkvist et al, 1998: 944). Another view mirrors some of the observations made in previous chapters and considers how haste to complete projects only serves to exacerbate their complexity thus lengthening lead time. For example, in Drummond's (1996, 1998, 1999) research on the Taurus stock exchange IT system one of the key features is the adoption of a very tight deadline (18 months) for the completion of a very large-scale project involving the installation of a state-of-the-art electronic share dealing system. (The project was abandoned in March, 1993 eighteen months after the original deadline had passed.) Drummond's study centred on the 'irrationality of rationality' and the respect that the technical managers in the Taurus case had for rational analysis. In contrast the 'gut feel' of managers in the group monitoring the project was that the project was going awry early on. However, they did not have the technical literacy to express their unease to the technical team whose detailed progress reports continually suggested that the required analyses had been done and that problems could be overcome. (Essentially, there was a lack of probing capacity on the part of the monitoring group managers.)

A further aspect of micro-politics that merits greater attention in future concerns the career aspirations of managers involved in major technology projects. For example, the association of career rewards with outcomes (rather than processes) seems to result in managers standing by their original decisions even when they are failing. Instead, managers gamble on their initial decision in the hope that they can make up for earlier losses. In contrast, to reverse or withdraw from the original commitment is regarded as unfavourable to career aspirations, constancy being more highly valued than being able to admit that one was mistaken (Boulding et al, 1997). Essentially, participation in radical innovation or large-scale technology ventures constitutes a means for managers to upgrade their reputation and ultimately their career prospects (Laurila, 1997). Moreover, career ambitions and functional background provide the backdrop for rivalry between individuals and groups, which may hinder development efforts. Such internal conflict has been identified in an ethnographic study of new product development conducted by Jones and Stevens (1999). In this study one key (sales) employee felt he was being passed over for promotion to the post of sales director in favour of another manager (an engineer) who he felt was inadequately qualified. The connection is made between the disaffection of the sales employee, the tension between him and the new sales director, inadequate understanding of the potential for attracting a volume market and the product design requirements related to different product-market positions (Jones and Stevens, 1999).

## The Social Construction of Large-scale Technology

The previous section referred to some temporal and interpretative aspects of decision-making and project management of significance to the management of large-scale technology projects. Now it is appropriate to return to the wider remit of the control of 'grand-scale' technology within society. As Chapter 1 considered, the focus on the 'control' of technology has been called into question recently, for owing too much to a modernist and 'naïve rationalist view of the possibility of controlling anything', and also in terms of the conception of what should count as 'good' or 'bad' technology (Coombs, 1995). Instead, it is argued, network perspectives analyze the parallel processes by which the creation and use of technology takes place in conjunction with the ongoing redefinition and reconstruction of the interests of individuals and groups comprising the relevant networks.

Where do incrementalism and the social control of technology, on which the work contained in this book has drawn heavily, stand with respect to these arguments? To take the point about control first, the application of incrementalist ideas to technology development owes much to the work of Langdon Winner, part of which addresses the argument that there is a loss of agency associated with technical complexity (Winner, 1977). In some quarters this strain of thinking has been interpreted as an analysis of technology 'out of control' (for example, by Rip et al, 1995). Work on the inflexibility of large-scale technology arguably has fed this impression, whereas the aspect of the research that seems most helpful to the management of technology in society concerns social learning (and interpretative flexibility) rather than 'rationalist' control. Where control has been expressed in terms of possibly too narrow an identification with objectives of particular promoters of a project (oil companies wishing to assert control over costs towards predetermined rates of return, for example) social learning suggests emergent decision-making or wider debate over ends and means. In the research presented here there is evidence of some problems of social learning, including processes by which debate becomes constrained or feedback appears to be difficult to integrate into future decisions.

There are implications of this work for the suggestion made by proponents of constructive technology assessment that 'creative incrementalism' should be practised. This proposal is made as a means to broaden the design criteria and range of actors involved in technology development, and so to enhance the potential for socially legitimate technology (Rip et al, 1995b). As outlined in Part I, the CTA approach emphasizes the decentralized, 'multi-actor' nature of technology; at least there are descriptive and prescriptive claims to this effect, which underpin the advocacy of creative incrementalism. However, in a sense CTA, as promoted by Rip and colleagues, could be attacked for advancing what its proponents would like to see to the neglect of an alternative analysis of the construction of technology as it occurs in practice. Sharing something in common with Lindblom's early work on incrementalism, and Quinn's on logical incrementalism, the focus prescriptively is on the multiplicity of actors who should be involved in decision-making and the inability of any central figure or authority to control affairs. Yet the different case studies presented here show that whilst a number of different parties play some role within decision-making (noting, as Winner (1991) does, that some influential ones may not be readily or neatly identified), the quality of access to or influence over policy differs markedly. Moreover the actors' dealings with each other are such that, in actor-network terms, the costs of translation may be great, as may be the partiality and instability of alignment and irreversibilization within the relevant actor networks (c.f. Callon, 1992). In short, to return again to a point made in Chapter 1, constructive technology assessment may turn out to be no more than a 'utopian dream' if its proponents cling to an over-optimistic view of pluralistic decision-making or fail to address the way in which alternative technological options are (prematurely) closed.

Future avenues for employing incrementalist, social control/learning and emerging constructive technology assessment approaches, in a complementary way, lie in identifying areas of misalignment between actors and in the relationship between politics and markets and technology development. As far as the progress of constructive approaches to technology development in society is concerned there are some interesting issues to be confronted. First, there seems to be a paradox of alignment. CTA emphasizes techniques such as consensus conferences as means to align actors and to facilitate social learning and the design of socially durable technology. However just as early versions of incrementalism were criticized for the potential for the building of a 'deceived consensus' (that is the idea that we can all agree to do the 'wrong' thing) so can such alignment between actors gained through the consensus building exercises suggested by CTA. One of the intriguing findings from Drummond's Taurus case study concerned the idea that attempting to accommodate a wide range of interests actually serves to complicate the process of design and hence exacerbates lead time and costs (Drummond, 1998). Such an observation seems to merit recognition in our considerations of the role of broader debate and social learning in technology development.

Similarly, what model(s) of power infuse thinking about the construction of technology? In the above case studies there is a recognition of 'nondecision-making', if not fully the hegemonic dimension of power suggested by Lukes. In the Channel Tunnel and wave power cases, for example, the underlying notion of power may be seen to be relational, to be conceived of in terms of the ongoing struggles between actors writing, rewriting or reinterpreting the rules of the game, or indeed the game (c.f. Clegg, 1989). No doubt this treatment of power could be made more sophisticated or explicit. In contrast, however, the advocacy of CTA seems to ignore these deeper-lying issues of the exercise or agenda-shaping expression of power, whilst at the same time idealizing agreement. This, as later work by Lindblom (1990: 292) asserts, 'creates obstacles to those social changes that do not win the assent of the advantaged'. In the cases presented above the analysis of the projects demonstrated alignment between certain influential actors at certain junctures but also the contested and latent conflicts of decision-making, both at the level of public policy and of inter-firm relations. The cases also speak indirectly to Callon's notion of irreversibilization, to illuminate how some technical and policy options are closed off. To some extent the cases point towards an emergent view of network relations, with the Channel Tunnel case study presenting a particularly dramatic story of problems associated with inter-organizational assertiveness, coordination and mutual distrust (c.f. Debresson and Amese's (1991) identification of the costs of networks as an under-researched area of study). As referred to above they do not deal directly with the more contemporary post-modern concepts of power wherein the individual manager's reputation for being in 'control', or being associated with grand projects constitutes and reinforces their identity. This is the kind of theme that needs to be developed in a new conception of the control and assessment of technology, if more finely grained analysis is to be achieved.

On the related topic of politics and markets CTA advises the adoption of forceful visions of the future and 'technology forcing', in conjunction with market measures to stimulate demand in strategic niches. Again, these measures are means to stimulate demand and social learning, for the promotion of socially useful technology (Rip et al, 1995b; Schot and Rip, 1997). Some relevant issues here pertain to the amount of 'negotiation space', or autonomy, that should be accorded to developers (Law and Callon, 1988) but also to the matter of how to avoid irreversibilities that may emerge due to a lack of prior support for alternative options (Callon, 1995). Comparing this with the approach to incrementalism presented above allows a number of comments to be made. Firstly, the advocacy of CTA may be argued to represent the type of relationship between means and ends long ago found wanting in the classical (or 'synoptic') model of rational decision-making. What underpins CTA is the anticipation of impacts, despite the disclaimer that 'impacts are co-produced' (Schot and Rip, 1997). The nature of technology forcing emphasizes the promotion of strong social visions to which technology development is directed. Arguably, some technologies – nuclear power springs to mind - that are now regarded as especially risky or potentially harmful are partly the product of strong social visions, considered to be socially benign and deserving of protection from market forces so as to enable development. In contrast, Lindblom's version of the incremental approach places greater reliance upon the ongoing remediation of social ills than the setting of high visions and the proactive search for opportunities.

In the field of technology policy, Morone and Woodhouse (1986; 1989), Collingridge (1992), while advocating an incremental approach see a more active role for policy-makers than is usually recognized. This relates to the search for trial and error strategies that 'attack egregious risks', for alternative options that circumvent potential risks and for what Lovins and Lovins (1982) refer to as resilient technical systems. Fundamentally, such an approach involves decision-makers being actively prepared to learn from mistakes that will inevitably occur, as distinct from expecting to be able to fully analyze all risks and costs in advance, or simply waiting for feedback on the performance of past decisions to arrive (Morone and Woodhouse, 1986; Collingridge, 1992). More specifically, the role of governmental agencies may be to ensure diversity two senses: diversity of access to policy making of 'counter-experts' to encourage 'competition of ideas' (Lindblom, 1990); and diversity of supply or distribution (to counter the privileged, often monopolistic, position of large corporations in sectors in which inflexible technologies are promoted). The degree to which the development of inflexible technology is identified with the influence of lobbies featuring large and powerful businesses is of concern to the extent that their closeness to central government enables them to win concessions that have the effect of diluting the operation of market mechanisms. This may result in the protection from financial risk of investments in technology that could be classed as socially undesirable or of penalizing investments in those technical options that may be safer or less wasteful of resources. This analysis of the links between policy, markets and technology development indicates some potential for complementarity of political decision-making and social constructionist approaches to understanding large-scale technology.

## References


Bart, C.K. (1999), 'Controlling New Products: a Contingency Approach', *International Journal of Technology Management*, vol. 18, pp. 395-413.

Boulding, W., Morgan, R. and Staelin, R. (1997), 'Pulling the Plug to Stop the New Product Drain', *Journal of Marketing Research*, vol. 34, pp. 164-176.

Callon, M. (1992), 'The Dynamics of Techno-economic Networks', in R. Coombs, P. Saviotti and V. Walsh (eds.), *Technological Change and Company Strategies*, Academic Press, London, pp. 72-102.

Callon, M. (1995), 'Technological Conception and Adoption Network: Lessons for the CTA Practitioner', in A. Rip, T.J. Misa, and J. Schot (eds.) *Managing Technology in Society: the Approach of Constructive Technology Assessment*, Pinter, London, pp. 307-329.

Clegg, S.R. (1989), *Frameworks of Power*, Sage, London.

Collingridge, D. (1980), *The Social Control of Technology*, Frances Pinter, London.

Collingridge, D. (1992), *The Management of Scale*, Routledge, London.

Coombs, R. (1995), 'Firm Strategies and Technical Choices', in A. Rip, T.J. Misa, and J. Schot (eds.) *Managing Technology in Society: the Approach of Constructive Technology Assessment*, Pinter, London, pp. 331-345.

Debresson, C. and Amese, F. (1991), 'Networks of Innovators: A Review and Introduction to the Issue', *Research Policy*, vol. 20, pp. 363-379.

Drummond, H. (1996), *Escalation in Decision-making: the Tragedy of Taurus*, Oxford University Press, Oxford.

Drummond, H. (1998), 'Is Escalation Always Irrational?', *Organization Studies*, vol. 19, pp. 911-929.

Drummond, H. (1999), 'Analysis and Intuition in Technological Choice: the Lessons of Taurus', *International Journal of Technology Management*, vol. 17, pp. 459-466.

Freeman, C. (1982), *The Economics of Industrial Innovation* (2nd edition), Frances Pinter, London.

Green, K. (1992), 'Creating Demand for Biotechnology: Shaping Technologies and Markets', in R. Coombs, P. Saviotti, P. and V. Walsh, *Technological Change and Company Strategies*, Academic Press, London, pp. 164-184.

Grint, K. and Woolgar, S. (1997), *The Machine at Work: Technology, Work and Organization*, Polity, London.

Grinyer, J., Russell, A. and Collinson, D. (1998), 'Evidence of Managerial Short-termism in the UK', *British Journal of Management*, vol. 9, pp. 13-22.

Hall, P. (1980), *Great Planning Disasters*, University of California Press, Berkeley, CA.

Hayes, R.H. and Garvin, D.A. (1982), 'Managing as if Tomorrow Mattered', *Harvard Business Review*, May-June, pp. 71-79.

Jacobs, M.T. (1991), *Short-term America*, Harvard Business School, Boston, MA.

Jones, O. and Stevens, G. (1999), 'Evaluating Failure in the Innovation Process: the Micropolitics of New Product Development', *R&D Management*, vol. 29, pp. 167-185.

Laurila, J. (1997), 'The Thin Line Between Advanced and Conventional New Technology: a Case Study on Paper Industry Management', *Journal of Management Studies*, vol. 34, pp. 219-239.

Law, J. and Callon, M. (1988), 'Engineering and Sociology in a Military Aircraft Project: a Network Analysis of Technological Change', *Social Problems*, vol. 35, pp. 284-297.

Lindblom, C.E. (1990), *Inquiry and Change*, Yale University Press, New York.

Lindkvist, L., Soderlund, J., and Tell, F. (1998), 'Managing Product Development Projects: On the Significance of Fountains and Deadlines', *Organization Studies*, vol. 19, pp. 931-951.

Lovins, A. and Lovins, G. (1982), *Brittle Power*, Brickhouse, Andover, MA.

Lukes, S. (1974), *Power: A Radical View*, Macmillan, London.

MacKenzie, D. (1992), 'Economic and Sociological Explanation of Technical Change', in R. Coombs, P. Saviotti, and V. Walsh, *Technological Change and Company Strategies*, Academic Press, London, pp. 25-48.

Molina, A. (1998), 'The Nature of 'Failure' in a Technological Initiative: the Case of the Europrocessor', *Technology Analysis and Strategic Management*, vol. 10, 1998, pp. 23-40.

Morone, J. and Woodhouse, E.J. (1986), *Averting Catastrophe: Strategies for Regulating Risky Technologies*, University California Press, Berkeley, CA.

Morris, P.W.G. and Hough, G. H. (1987), *The Anatomy of Major Projects: A Study of the Reality of Project Management*, John Wiley, Chichester.

Rip, A., Misa, T.J. and Schot, J. (1995b), 'Epilogue', in A. Rip, T.J. Misa and J. Schot (eds.) *Managing Technology in Society: the Approach of Constructive Technology Assessment*, Pinter, London, pp. 331-345.

Schilling, M. (1998), 'Technological Lock-out: an Integrative Model of the Economic and Strategic Factors Driving Technology Success and Failure, *Academy of Management Review*, vol. 23, pp. 267-285.

Schot, J. and Rip, A. (1997), 'The Past and Future of Constructive Technology Assessment', *Technological Forecasting and Social Change*, vol. 54, pp. 251-268.

Shapira, Z. and Berndt, D.J. (1997), 'Managing Grand-scale Construction Projects: A Risk-taking Perspective', *Research in Organizational Behaviour*, vol. 19, pp. 303-360.

SPRU (Science Policy Research Unit) (1972), *Success and Failure in Industrial Innovation*, Centre for the Study of Industrial Innovation, London.

Wildavsky, A. (1987), *Speaking Truth to Power: the Art and Craft of Policy Analysis*, Transaction Books New Brunswick, NJ.

Winner, L. (1977), *Autonomous Technology: Technics out of Control as a Theme in Political Thought*, MIT, Cambridge, MA.

Winner, L. (1991), 'Upon Opening the Black Box and Finding it Empty: Social Constructivism and the Philosophy of Technology', in J.C. Pitt and E. Lugo (eds.), *The Technology of Discovery and the Discovery of Technology*, Proceedings of the Sixth

International Conference of the Society for Philosophy and Technology, Blacksurg, pp. 503-519.

Wynne, B. (1995), 'Technology Assessment and Reflexive Social Learning: Observations From the Risk Field', in A. Rip, T.J. Misa and J. Schot (eds.), *Managing Technology in Society: the Approach of Constructive Technology Assessment*, Pinter, London, pp. 19-36.

Wynne, B. (1996), 'Misunderstood Misunderstandings: Social Identities and Public Uptake of Science', in A. Irwin and B. Wynne (eds.), *Misunderstanding Science? The Public Reconstruction of Science and Technology*, Cambridge, Cambridge University Press, pp. 19-46.

# Bibliography

Anderson, G. and Roskrow, B. (1994), *The Channel Tunnel Story*, E. and F.N. Spon, London.

Anonymous (1987), 'First Oil for Alwyn North', *Petroleum Times*, December, p. 10.

Arrow, K. (1964), 'Review of: A Strategy of Decision: Policy Evaluation as a Social Process', *Political Science Quarterly*, vol. 79, pp. 584-588.

Bachrach, P. and Baratz, M. (1962), 'Two Faces of Power', *American Political Science Review*, vol. 56, pp. 947-952.

Balogh, Lord (1974), 'The North Sea Oil Blunder', *The Banker*, vol. 124, pp. 281-288.

Bart, C.K. (1999), 'Controlling New Products: a Contingency Approach', *International Journal of Technology Management*, vol. 18, pp. 395-413.

Bedelian, H. (1995), *Lessons From a Major BOT (Build, Own, Transfer) Project: the Channel Tunnel*, Transcript of a presentation to Portsmouth University, Portsmouth, 15 June 1995.

Benard, A. and Morton, A. (1989), 'The Private Sector Financing of the Channel Tunnel', in Institution of Civil Engineers, *The Channel Tunnel*, Thomas Telford, London.

Benn, T. (1980), *Arguments for Socialism*, Penguin, Harmondsworth.

Bijker, W.E, Hughes, T.P. and Pinch, T.J. (1987), 'Introduction', in W.E. Bijker, T.P. Hughes, and T.J. Pinch, (eds.), *The Social Construction of Technological Systems: New Directions in the Sociology and History of Technology*, MIT Press, Cambridge, Mass., pp. 11-15.

Boulding, W., Morgan, R. and Staelin, R. (1997), 'Pulling the Plug to Stop the New Product Drain', *Journal of Marketing Research*, vol. 34, pp. 164-176.

Bowen, M.G. (1987), 'The Escalation Phenomenon Reconsidered: Decision Dilemma or Decision Errors ?' *Academy of Management Review*, vol. 12, pp. 52-66.

Braybrooke, D. and Lindblom, C.E. (1963), *A Strategy of Decision: Policy Evaluation as a Social Process,* Free Press, New York.

Callon, M. (1986), 'The Sociology of an Actor-Network: the Case of the Electric Vehicle, in M. Callon, J. Law, and A. Rip (eds.), *Mapping the Dynamics of Science and Technology*, Macmillan, London.

Callon, M. (1987), 'Society in the Making: the Study of Technology as a Tool for Sociological Analysis', in W.E. Bijker, T.P. Hughes, and T.J. Pinch, (eds.), *The Social Construction of Technological Systems: New Directions in the Sociology and History of Technology*, MIT Press, Cambridge, Mass., pp. 83-103.

Callon, M. (1992), 'The Dynamics of Techno-economic Networks', in R. Coombs, P. Saviotti and V. Walsh (eds.), *Technological Change and Company Strategies*, Academic Press, London, pp. 72-102.

Callon, M. (1995), 'Technological Conception and Adoption Network: Lessons for the CTA Practitioner', in A. Rip, T.J. Misa, and J. Schot (eds.) *Managing Technology in Society: the Approach of Constructive Technology Assessment*, Pinter, London, pp. 307-329.

Carley, M. (1980), *Rational Techniques in Policy Analysis*, Heinemann Educational Books, London.

Clegg, S.R. (1989), *Frameworks of Power*, Sage, London.

Collingridge, D. (1980), *The Social Control of Technology*, Frances Pinter, London.

Collingridge, D. (1982), *Critical Decision Making: a New Theory of Social Choice*, Frances Pinter, London.

Collingridge, D. (1983), *Technology in the Policy Process: Controlling Nuclear Power*, Frances Pinter, London.

Collingridge, D. (1989, 11 November), *Personal correspondence*.

Collingridge, D. (1990), 'Technology, Organizations and Incrementalism; the Space Shuttle', *Technology Analysis and Strategic Management*, vol. 2, pp. 181-200.

Collingridge, D. (1992), *The Management of Scale*, Routledge, London.

Collingridge, D., Genus, A. and James, P. (1994), 'Inflexibility in the Development of North Sea Oil', *Technological Forecasting and Social Change*, vol. 45, pp. 169-188.

Collingridge, D. and James, P. (1989 a), *Technology, Organizations and Incrementalism Large Irrigation Schemes in Developing Countries*, working paper as part of the Diseconomies of Scale In Production Systems Project carried out jointly by Aston and Warwick Universities and funded by the Leverhulme Foundation.

Collingridge, D. and James, P. (1989 b), 'Technology, Organizations and Incrementalism: High Rise System Building in the UK', *Technology Analysis and Strategic Management*, vol. 1, pp. 79-97.

Coombs, R. (1995), 'Firm Strategies and Technical Choices', in A. Rip, T.J. Misa, and J. Schot, (eds.) *Managing Technology in Society: the Approach of Constructive Technology Assessment*, Pinter, London, pp. 331-345.

County NatWest Woodmac (1989, and various dates), *North Sea Service*, National Westminster Investment Bank Group, Edinburgh.

Craven-Walker, A. (1973), 'How B.P. will Equip the North Sea's Forties Field', *World Oil*, no. 176, 6 May, pp. 55-58.

Debresson, C. and Amese, F. (1991), 'Networks of Innovators: A Review and Introduction to the Issue, *Research Policy*, vol. 20, pp. 363-379.

Department of Energy (various annual editions), *Development of the Oil and Gas Resources of the United Kingdom*, HMSO, London.

Department of Energy (1976), *North Sea Costs Escalation Study*, Energy Paper no. 7, HMSO, London.

Department of Energy (1978), *Energy Policy: A Consultative Document*, HMSO, London.

Department of Energy (1985), *Wave Energy - The Department of Energy R&D Programme 1974-1983*, ETSU, Harwell.

Department of Energy (1989), *Development of the Oil and Gas Resources of the United Kingdom*, HMSO, London.

Department of Energy (1990), *Development of the Oil and Gas Resources of the United Kingdom*, HMSO, London.

DETR (Department of Environment, Transport and the Regions) (2000), *Press Briefing*, no. 407, 8 June.

Douglas, M. and Wildavsky, A. (1982), *Risk and Culture: an Essay on the Selection of Environmental Dangers*, University of California Press, Los Angeles, California.

Dror, Y. (1964), 'Muddling Through – Science or Inertia', *Public Administration Review*, vol. 24, pp. 153-157.

Drummond, H. (1996), *Escalation in Decision-making: the Tragedy of Taurus*, Oxford University Press, Oxford.

Drummond, H. (1998), 'Is Escalation Always Irrational?', *Organization Studies*, vol. 19, pp. 911-929.

Drummond, H. (1999), 'Analysis and Intuition in Technological Choice: the Lessons of Taurus', *International Journal of Technology Management*, vol. 17, pp. 459-466.

DTI (1999a), *New and Renewable Energy: Prospects for the 21st Century*, www.dti.gov.uk/renew/condoc.

DTI (1999b), *A Fair Deal for Consumer: Modernising the Framework for Utility Regulation – Regulatory, Environmental and Equal Treatment Appraisals*, www.dti.gov.uk/urt.

Elliott, D. (1992), 'Renewables and the Privatisation of the UK ESI', *Energy Policy*, vol. 20, pp. 257-68.

Etzioni, A. (1967), 'Mixed Scaninng: A 'Third' Approach in Decision-making', *Public Administration*, vol. 27, pp. 385-392.

Eurotunnel (1987), *Eurotunnel Prospectus*, Eurotunnel, London and Paris.

Eurotunnel (1990), *Eurotunnel Rights Issue*, Eurotunnel, London and Paris.

Eurotunnel (1994), *Eurotunnel Rights Issue*, Eurotunnel, London and Paris.

Eurotunnel (1995a), *Annual Report, 1994*, Eurotunnel, London and Paris.

Eurotunnel (1995b), *Progress Report*, Eurotunnel, London and Paris.

Eurotunnel (2000), *Annual Report, 2000*, Eurotunnel, London and Paris.

Falnes, J. and Lovseth, J. (1991), 'Ocean Wave Energy', *Energy Policy*, vol. 19, pp. 768-775.

Fetters, J.K. (1971), 'Here's What Phillips Learned About Drilling in the North Sea', *Oil and Gas Journal*, vol. 69, 9 August, pp. 76-86.

Fier, G.D. (1972), 'The Next Exploration Technique in the North Sea', *Oil and Gas Journal,* vol. 70, 10 April, p. 160.

Fisher, J. (1993), 'Industrial relations and the construction of the Channel Tunnel', *Industrial Relations Journal*, vol. 24, pp. 211-225.

Flood, M. (1991), *Energy Without End,* Friends of the Earth, London.

Flood, M., Conroy, C. and Gordon, D. (1982), *Eclipse of the Sun? The Future of Renewable Energy Research in Britain,* Friends of the Earth, London.

Freeman, C. (1982), *The Economics of Industrial Innovation* (2nd ed.), Frances Pinter, London.

Genus, A. (1995), *Flexible Strategic Management*, Chapman and Hall, London.

Green, K. (1992), 'Creating Demand for Biotechnology: Shaping Technologies and Markets', in R. Coombs, P. Saviotti, and V. Walsh, *Technological Change and Company Strategies*, Academic Press, London, pp. 164-184.

Grint, K. and Woolgar, S. (1997), *The Machine at Work: Technology, Work and Organization*, Polity, London.

Grinyer, J. Russell, A. and Collinson, D. (1998), 'Evidence of Managerial Short-termism in the UK', *British Journal of Management*, vol. 9, pp. 13-22.

Grubb, M. (1990), 'The Cinderella Options a Study of Modernized Renewable Energy Technologies: Part 2 Political and Policy Analysis', *Energy Policy,* vol. 18, pp. 711-725.

Grubb, M. (1991), 'The Integration of Renewable Electricity Sources', *Energy Policy*, vol. 18, pp. 670-688.

Hagerman, G.M. and Heller, T. (1988), 'Wave Energy: a Survey of Twelve Near-term Technologies', *Proceedings of the International Renewable Energy Conference*, Honolulu, HI, 18-24 September, pp. 98-110.

Hall, P. (1980), *Great Planning Disasters*, University of California Press, Berkeley, CA.

Hamlett, P. (1991), *The Political Construction of Technology*, Personal memorandum, December.

Hann, D. (1986), 'The Process of Government and UK Oil Participation Policy, *Energy Policy*, vol. 14, pp. 253-261.

Harrigan, K.R. (1985), *Strategic Flexibility*, Lexington, Lexington, Mass.

Hayes, R.H. and Garvin, D.A. (1982), 'Managing as if Tomorrow Mattered', *Harvard Business Review*, May-June, pp. 71-79.

Heaney, J. (1973), 'Development of Auk and Brent', *Petroleum Review,* vol. 27, pp. 259-264.

Hill, S. (1988), *The Tragedy of Technology: Human Liberation Versus Domination in the Late Twentieth Century*, Pluto, London.

Holliday, I. (1989), *Privatizing Transport Infrastructure: The Politics of Channel Tunnel Concession*, The Channel Tunnel Research Unit, University of Kent.

House of Commons Energy Committee (1984), *Ninth Report from the Energy Committee Session 1983-84, Energy Research, Development and Demonstration in the United Kingdom*, H.M.S.O, London.

House of Commons Energy Committee (1987) *Session 1986/87, The Effect of Oil and Gas Prices on Activity in the North Sea*, HMSO, London.

House of Commons Energy Committee (1992), *Renewable Energy*, HMSO, London.

Howell, D. (1980), *Hansard*, 23 July.

Hughes, T. (1983), *Networks of Power: Electrification in Western Society: 1880-1930*, John Hopkins University Press, Baltimore, Maryland.

Hughes, T. (1987), 'The Evolution of Large-scale Technological Systems', in W.E. Bijker, T.P. Hughes, and T.J. Pinch, (eds.), *The Social Construction of Technological Systems: New Directions in the Sociology and History of Technology*, MIT Press, Cambridge, Mass., pp. 50-82.

IEA (International Energy Agency) (1991), *Energy Policies of IEA Countries, 1990 Review*, OECD, Paris.

*The Independent* (1989), 26 May.

*The Independent* (1995), 15 September.

Jacobs, M.T. (1991), *Short-term America*, Harvard Business School, Boston, MA.

Jarillo, J.C. (1988), 'On Strategic Networks', *Strategic Management Journal*, vol. 9, pp. 31-41.

Jeffrey, J. (1990), 'Dirty Tricks: How the Nuclear Lobby Stopped the Development of Wave Power in Britain', *The Ecologist*, vol. 20, pp. 85-90.

Johnson, G. (1987), *Strategic Change and the Management Process*, Blackwell, Oxford.

Johnston, R. (1985), 'The Social Character of Technology: Reply to Collingridge', *Social Studies of Science*, vol. 15, pp. 381-383.

Jones, B. (1987), *The Tunnel, The Channel and Beyond*, Ellis Horwood, London.

Jones, C.O. (1975), *Clean Air: the Policies and Politics of Pollution Control*, University of Pittsburgh Press, Pittsburgh.

Jones, O. and Stevens, G. (1999), 'Evaluating Failure in the Innovation Process: the Micropolitics of New Product Development', *R&D Management*, vol. 29, pp. 167-185.

Jorgensen, U. and Karnoe, P. (1995) 'The Danish Wind-Turbine Story: Technical Solutions to Political Visions', in A. Rip, T.J. Misa, and J. Schot, *Managing Technology in Society: the Approach of Constructive Technology Assessment*, Pinter, London, pp. 57-81.

Kanter, R.M. (1989), *When Giants Learn to Dance*, Unwin, London.

Kennedy, J.L. (1974), 'North Sea Report', *Oil and Gas Journal*, vol. 72, 3 June, pp. 200-202.

Kirkland, C. (1995), 'The Channel Tunnel - lessons learned', *Tunnelling and Underground Space Technology*, vol. 10, pp. 5-6.

Lampel, J., Miller, R., and Floricel, S. (1996), 'Information Assymetries and Technological Innovation in Large Engineering Construction Projects', *R&D Management*, vol. 26, pp. 357-369.

Laurila, J. (1997), 'The Thin Line Between Advanced and Conventional New Technology: a Case Study on Paper Industry Management', *Journal of Management Studies*, vol. 34, pp. 219-239.

Law, J. and Callon, M. (1988), 'Engineering and Sociology in a Military Aircraft Project: a Network Analysis of Technological Change', *Social Problems*, vol. 35, pp. 284-297.

Lemley, J. (1995), 'Managing the Channel Tunnel - lessons learned', *Tunnelling and Underground Space Technology*, vol. 10, pp. 9-11.

Lewis, T. (1985), *Wave Energy*, Graham and Trotman, London.

Lindblom, C.E. (1959), 'The Science of Muddling Through', *Public Administration Review*, vol. 19, pp. 79-88.

Lindblom, C.E. (1968), *The Policy-making Process*, Prentice-Hall, New Jersey.

Lindblom, C.E. (1977), *Politics and Markets*, Basic Books, New York.

Lindblom, C.E. (1979), 'Still muddling not yet through', *Public Administration Review*, vol. 39, pp. 517-527.

Lindblom, C.E. (1980), *The Policy Making Process* (2nd edition), Prentice-Hall, New Jersey.

Lindblom, C.E. (1989, 4 October), *Personal correspondence*.

Lindblom, C.E. (1990), *Inquiry and Change*, Yale University Press, New Haven.

Lindblom, C.E. and Woodhouse, E.J. (1993), *The Policy Making Process* (3rd ed.), Prentice-Hall, New Jersey.

Lindkvist, L., Soderlund, J., and Tell, F. (1998), 'Managing Product Development Projects: On the Significance of Fountains and Deadlines', *Organization Studies*, vol. 19, pp. 931-951.

Lovins, A. and Lovins, G. (1982), *Brittle Power*, Brickhouse, Andover, MA.

Lowi, T. (1970), 'Decision-making vs. Policy-making: Toward An Antidote for Technocracy', *Public Administration Review*, vol. 30, pp. 314-325.

Lukes, S. (1974), *Power: A Radical View*, Macmillan, London.

Lustick, I. (1980), 'Explaining theVariable Utility of Disjointed Incrementalism', *American Political Science Review*, vol. 74, pp. 442-453.

Lynch, J.F. (1965), 'North Sea Poses New Problems in Pipeline Engineering', *Oil and Gas Journal*, vol. 63, 2 August, pp. 113-116.

Lynk, E. (1988), 'The Depletion of UK North Sea Oil', *Scottish Journal of Political Economy*, vol. 35, pp. 313-333.

Mackay, D. I. and Mackay, G.A. (1975), *The Political Economy of North Sea Oil*, Martin Robertson, London.

MacKenzie, D. (1992), 'Economic and Sociological Explanation of Technical Change', in R. Coombs, Saviotti, P. and Walsh, V., *Technological Change and Company Strategies*, Academic Press, London, pp. 25-48.

MacKenzie, D. and Wacjman, J. (eds.) (1985), *The Social Shaping of Technology*, Open University, Buckingham.

Marcou, G. (1993), 'Public and private sectors in the delivery of public infrastructure: the case of the Channel Tunnel from an international perspective', *Environment and Planning C: Government and Policy* vol. 11, pp. 1-18.

Miller, D. (1992), *The Icarus Paradox*, Harper Business, New York, NY.

Mintzberg, H. and Waters, J. (1990), 'Does Decision Get in the Way?', *Organization Studies*, vol. 11, pp. 1-6.

Molina, A. (1998), 'The Nature of 'Failure' in a Technological Initiative: the Case of the Europrocessor', *Technology Analysis and Strategic Management*, vol. 10, 1998, pp. 23-40.

Morone, J. and Woodhouse, E.J. (1986), *Averting Catastrophe: Strategies for Regulating Risky Technologies*, University of California Press, Berkeley, CA.

Morone, J. and Woodhouse, E.J. (1989), *The Demise of Nuclear Energy, Lessons for Democratic Control of Technology*, Yale University Press, New Haven, Connecticut.

Morris, P.W.G. and Hough, G.H. (1987), The Anatomy of Major Projects, *A Study of the Reality of Project Management*, John Wiley, Chichester.

Morton, A. (1995a), *Transcript of Speech to EC Banks in the City*, London, 20 October.

Mort, M. (1995), 'Constructing Trident, Reinforcing the Network', *Technology Analysis and Strategic Management*, vol. 7, pp. 307-313.

Morton, A. (1995b), 'In-built conflicts resolved at a price', *International Railway Journal*, May, pp. 10-11.

National Audit Office (2000), *Ministry of Defence Major Project Report 1999*, Stationery Office, London.

National Engineering Laboratory (1976), *The Development of Wave Power - A Techno-economic Study*, NEL, Glasgow.

Neerhout, J. (1994), cited in: V. Fairweather, The Channel Tunnel: Larger than Life, and Late, *Civil Engineering*, May, pp. 42-46.

Noreng, O. (1980), *The Oil Industry and Government Strategy in the North Sea*, Croom Helm, London.

Odell, P. (1986), *Oil And World Power* (8th edition), Penguin, London.

Odell, P. and Rosing, K. (1977), 'Optimal Development of the North Sea's Oil Fields - Reply (to the Critique of Wall *et al.)*', *Energy Policy*, vol. 5, p. 305.

Odell, P. and Rosing, K. (1980), *The Future of Oil*, Kogan Page, London.

Pettigrew, A. (1990), 'Studying Strategic Choice and Strategic Change: A Comment on Mintzberg and Waters: Does Decision Get in the Way?', *Organization Studies*, vol. 1, pp. 6-11.

Pettigrew, A. and Whipp, R. (1991), *Managing Change for Competitive Success*, Blackwell, Oxford.

Pinch, T.J. and Bijker, W.E. (1987), 'The Social Construction of Facts and Artifacts: Or How the Sociology of Science and the Sociology of Technology Might Benefit Each Other', in W.E. Bijker, T.P. Hughes, and T.J. Pinch, (eds.), *The Social Construction of Technological Systems: New Directions in the Sociology and History of Technology*, MIT Press, Cambridge, MA, pp. 17-50.

Quinn, J.B. (1980), *Strategies for Change: Logical Incrementalism*, Irwin, Homewood, Ill.

Rajagopalan, N. and Rasheed, A.M.A. (1995), 'Incremental Models of Policy Formulation and Non-incremental Changes: Critical Review and Synthesis', *British Journal of Management*, vol. 6, pp. 289-302.

Ratzer, P. (1995), 'Lessons from Eurotunnel', *Project Finance International*, vol. 70, pp. 28-29.

Reid, R.G. (1987), 'A View of European Oil and Gas Issues', in J. Rees and P. Odell (eds.), *The International Oil Industry*, Macmillan, London, pp. 76-87.

Rip, A., Misa, T.J. and Schot, J. (1995a), 'Constructive Technology Assessment: A New Paradigm for Managing Technology in Society', in A. Rip, T.J. Misa, and J. Schot, *Managing Technology in Society: the Approach of Constructive Technology Assessment*, Pinter, London, pp. 1-12.

Rip, A., Misa, T.J. and Schot, J. (1995b), 'Epilogue', in A. Rip, T.J. Misa, and J. Schot (eds.) *Managing Technology in Society: the Approach of Constructive Technology Assessment*, Pinter, London, pp. 331-345.

Robbins, R. (1995), 'Boring Under the Channel: One Perspective on the Experience', *Tunnelling and Underground Space Technology*, vol. 10, pp. 23-25.

Robinson, C. (1981), 'The Errors of North Sea Policy', *Lloyds Bank Review*, no. 141, pp. 14-33.

Robinson, C. (1982), 'Oil Depletion Policy in the United Kingdom', *Three Banks Review*, no. 135, pp. 8-15.

Robinson, C. (1990), 'Successes and Failures in British Government North Sea Policy', paper presented at *25 Years of the North Sea*, Conference at Surrey University, 23 March.

Robinson, C. and Morgan, J. (1978), *North Sea Oil in the Future*, Macmillan, London.

Salter, S. (1988),'World Progress in Wave Energy 1988', *International Journal Of Ambient Energy*, vol. 10, pp. 3-24.

Sampson, A. (1988), *The Seven Sisters* (2nd ed.), Coronet, London.

Schilling, M. (1998), 'Technological Lock-out: an Integrative Model of the Economic and Strategic Factors Driving Technology Success and Failure', *Academy of Management Review*, vol. 23, pp. 267-285.

Schot, J. and Rip, A. (1997), 'The Past and Future of Constructive Technology Assessment', *Technological Forecasting and Social Change*, vol. 54, pp. 251-268.

Schulman, P.R. (1975), 'Non-incremental Policy Making: Notes Toward an Alternative Paradigm', *American Political Science Review*, vol. 69, pp. 1354-1370.

Scott, R.W. (1972), 'The North Sea: Offshore's Greatest Venture', *World Oil*, 15 August, pp. 33-40 and pp. 136-139.

Shapira, Z. and Berndt, D.J. (1997), 'Managing Grand-scale Construction Projects: A Risk-taking Perspective, *Research in Organizational Behaviour*, vol. 19, pp. 303-360.

Sharfman, M. and Dean, J.W. (1997), 'Flexibility in Strategic Decision-making: Informational and Ideological Perspectives', *Journal of Management Studies*, vol. 34, pp. 191-216.

Smith, W. (1991), 'Counting the Cost', *Newsletter of the Network for Alternative Technology and Technology Assessment*, vol. 72, pp. 18-19.

Soete, L. (1995), 'Constructive Technology Assessment: an Economic Perspective', in A. Rip, T.J. Misa and J. Schot, *Managing Technology in Society: the Approach of Constructive Technology Assessment*, Pinter, London, pp. 37-51.

SPRU (Science Policy Research Unit) (1972), *Success and Failure in Industrial Innovation*, Centre for the Study of Industrial Innovation, London.

Stannard, C.J. (1990), 'Managing a Mega-project - the Channel Tunnel', *Long Range Planning*, vol. 23, pp. 49-62.

Staw, B.M. and Ross, J. (1987), 'Behaviour in Escalation Situations: Antecedents, Prototypes and solutions', in L.L. Cummings and B.M. Staw, (eds.), *Research in Organization Behaviour*, JAI Press, London, pp. 39-78.

Steward, F. (1995), 'Risk Analysis and Rival Technical Trajectories: Consumer Safety in Bread and Butter', in A. Rip, T.J. Misa and J. Schot, *Managing Technology in Society: the Approach of Constructive Technology Assessment*, Pinter, London, pp. 111-135.

Stinchcombe, A.L. and Heimer, C. A. (1985), *Organization Theory and Project Management*, Norwegian University Press, Oslo.

Thorelli, H. (1986), 'Networks: Between Markets and Hierarchies', *Strategic Management Journal*, vol. 7, pp. 37-51.

Trimble, N. (1976), 'The Costs of North Sea Oil Developments: Past Trends and Future Prospects', *North Sea Occasional Paper No. 10*, University of Aberdeen Department of Political Economy, Aberdeen.

UKOOA (United Kingdom Offshore Operators' Association) (1999), *Oil and Gas: Economic Contribution - 1999 Economic Report*, www.ukooa.co.uk.

Vickerman, R. (1989), *The Private Provision of Infrastructure: The Channel Tunnel Project*, The Channel Tunnel Research Unit, University of Kent.

Vickerman, R. (1991), *Financing the Channel Tunnel*, The Channel Tunnel Research Unit, University of Kent.

Vickerman, R. (1994), *The Channel Tunnel: The Case for Private Sector Provision of Public Infrastructure?* The Channel Tunnel Research Unit, Kent University.

Wildavsky, A. (1987), *Speaking Truth to Power: the Art and Craft of Policy Analysis*, Transaction Books, New Brunswick, NJ.

Wildavsky, A. and Tannenbaum, E. (1981), *The Politics of Mistrust*, Sage, London.

Williamson, O.E. (1975), *Markets and Hierarchies: Analysis and Anti-trust Implications*, Free Press, New York.

Winner, L. (1977), *Autonomous Technology: Technics out of Control as a Theme in Political Thought*, MIT, Cambridge, MA.

Winner, L. (1991), 'Upon Opening the Black Box and Finding it Empty: Social Constructivism and the Philosophy of Technology', in J.C. Pitt, and E. Lugo, (eds.), *The Technology of Discovery and the Discovery of Technology*,

Proceedings of the Sixth International Conference of the Society for Philosophy and Technology, Blacksurg, pp. 503-519.

Wynne, B. (1995), 'Technology Assessment and Reflexive Social Learning: Observations From the Risk Field', in A. Rip, T.J. Misa and J. Schot, *Managing Technology in Society: the Approach of Constructive Technology Assessment*, Pinter, London, 1995, pp. 19-36.

Wynne, B. (1996) 'Misunderstood Misunderstandings: Social Identities and Public Uptake of Science', in A. Irwin, and B. Wynne, (eds.), *Misunderstanding Science? The Public Reconstruction of Science and Technology*, Cambridge University Press, Cambridge, pp. 19-46.

# Index